CREATION'S COUPLE

By
Ellen G. White

TEACH Services, Inc.
Brushton, New York

2006 07 08 09 10 11 12 · 5 4 3 2 1

Copyright © 2006 TEACH Services, Inc.
ISBN-13: 978-1-57258-427-3
ISBN-10: 1-57258-427-0
Library of Congress Control Number: 2006933353

Published by

TEACH Services, Inc.
www.TEACHServices.com

CONTENTS

Chapter 1

CREATION

After the earth was created, and the beasts upon it, the Father and Son carried out their purpose, which was designed before the fall of Satan, to make man in their own image. They had wrought together in the creation of the earth and every living thing upon it. And now God says to his Son, "Let us make man in our image." As Adam came forth from the hand of his Creator, he was of noble height, and of beautiful symmetry. He was more than twice as tall as men now living upon earth, and was well proportioned. His features were perfect and beautiful. His complexion was neither white, nor sallow, but ruddy, glowing with the rich tint of health. Eve was not quite as tall as Adam. Her head reached a little above his shoulders. She, too, was noble—perfect in symmetry, and very beautiful.—*Spiritual Gifts*, Vol. 3, p. 33, par. 2.

The Lord created man out of the dust of the earth. He made Adam a partaker of His life, His nature. There was breathed into him the breath of the Almighty, and he became a living soul. Adam was perfect in form—strong, comely, pure, bearing the image of his Maker. God gave him a companion, a wife, to share with him the beauties of nature.—*Manuscript Releases*, Vol. 10, p. 326, par. 4.

God is a being, and man was made in His image. After God created man in His image, the form was perfect in all its arrangements, but it had no vitality. Then a personal, self-existing God breathed into that form the breath of life, and man became a living, breathing, intelligent being. All parts of the human machinery were put in motion. The heart, the arteries, the veins, the tongue, the hands, the feet, the perceptions of the mind, the senses, were placed under physical law. It was then that man became a living soul.—*Manuscript Releases*, Vol. 3, p. 304, par. 1.

The Lord made man upright in the beginning. He was created with a perfectly balanced mind. The size and strength of the organs of the mind were perfectly developed. Adam was a perfect type of man. Every quality of mind was well proportioned, each having a distinctive office, and yet dependent one upon another for the full and proper use of any one of them...—"Experience as a Teacher," *Advent Review and Sabbath Herald*, 7-27-86, par. 3.

Created to be "the image and glory of God" (1 Corinthians 11:7), Adam and Eve had received endowments not unworthy of their high destiny. Graceful and symmetrical in form, regular and beautiful in feature, their countenances glowing with the tint of health and the light of joy and hope, they bore in outward resemblance the likeness of their Maker. Nor was this likeness manifest in the physical nature only. Every faculty of mind and soul reflected the Creator's glory. Endowed with high mental and spiritual gifts, Adam and Eve were made but "little lower than the angels" (Hebrews 2:7), that they might not only discern the wonders of the visible universe, but comprehend moral responsibilities and obligations.—*Education*, p. 20, par. 2.

Adam and Eve came forth from the hand of their Creator in the perfection of every physical, mental, and spiritual endowment. God planted for them a garden, and surrounded them with everything lovely and attractive to the eye, and that which their physical necessities required. This holy pair looked out upon a world of unsurpassed loveliness and glory. A benevolent Creator had given them evidences of his goodness and love in providing them with fruits, vegetables, and grains, and had caused to grow out of the ground trees of every variety for usefulness and beauty.—"Redemption, No. 1," *Second Advent Review and Sabbath Herald*, 2-24-74, par. 4.

Adam was crowned as king in Eden. To him was given dominion over every living thing that God had created. The Lord blessed Adam and Eve with intelligence such as he had not given to the animal creation. He made Adam the rightful sovereign over all the works of his hands. Man made in the divine image could contemplate and appreciate the glorious works of God in nature.—"Redemption, No. 1," *Second Advent Review and Sabbath Herald*, 02-24-74, par. 6.

Angels on probation had been deceived by Satan, and had been led on by him in the great rebellion in Heaven against Christ. They failed to bear the test brought to bear upon them, and they fell. Adam was then created in the image of God and placed upon probation. He had a perfectly developed organism. All his faculties harmonized. In all his emotions, words, and actions there was a perfect conformity to the will of his Maker. After God had made every provision for the happiness of man, and had supplied his every want, he tested Adam's loyalty. If the holy pair should be obedient, the race would after a time be made equal to the angels. As Adam and Eve failed to bear this test, Christ proposed to become a voluntary offering for man.—"Redemption, No. 1," *Second Advent Review and Sabbath Herald*, 02-24-74, par. 26.

Man was made for happiness, not to be kept in continual worry. At his creation man was perfectly happy. The garden of Eden was an emblem of heaven and the love of God. The flowers exhibited their beauty and loveliness, ever giving out a fragrance grateful to the senses. Fruit trees bore their burden of precious treasures for the good of man. On every tree the birds caroled forth their songs of praise to God. In their untainted purity Adam and Eve delighted to listen to these glad songs of praise.—*Manuscript Releases*, Vol. 10, p. 241, par. 2.

In the varied lines of Christ's work, each part depends on the other part. God has made provision for reciprocal action and mutual relation of all animated beings. He has made arrangements that all shall be connected together, and the whole to God. No one can be dropped out of the Lord's plan without affecting the whole. Nothing is independent of the rest. In creating Adam and Eve as our parents, God designed that each human being should stand related to the rest, to be a part of the web of humanity.—*Manuscript Releases*, Vol. 5, p. 369, par. 1.

Adam was appointed by God to be monarch of the world, under the supervision of the Creator. "God said, Let us make man in Our image, after our likeness, and let him have dominion over the fish of the sea, and over the fowl of the air, and over the cattle, and over all the earth, and over every creeping thing that creepeth upon the earth. So God created man in His own image, in the image of God created He him." "The Lord God formed man of the dust of the ground, and breathed into his nostrils the breath of life; and man became a living soul....And the Lord God said, It is not good that the man should be alone; I will make him an helpmeet for him....And the Lord God caused a deep sleep to fall upon Adam, and he slept; and He took one of his ribs, and closed up the flesh instead thereof; and the rib, which the Lord God had taken from man, made He a woman, and brought her unto the man. And Adam said, This is now bone of my bone, and flesh of my flesh; she shall be called Woman, because she was taken out of Man. Therefore shall a man leave his father and his mother, and shall cleave unto his wife; and they shall be one flesh."—"The Marriage in Cana of Galilee," *The Signs of the Times*, 8-30-99, par. 2.

God Himself gave Adam a companion. He provided "an help meet for him"—a helper corresponding to him—one who was fitted to be his companion, and who could be one with him in love and sympathy. Eve was created from a rib taken from the side of Adam, signifying that she was not to control him as the head, nor to be trampled under his feet as an inferior, but to stand by his side as an equal, to be loved and protected by him. A part of man, bone of his bone, and flesh of his flesh, she was his second self; showing the close union and the affectionate attachment that should exist in this relation. "For no man ever yet hated his own flesh; but nourisheth and cherisheth it." "Therefore shall a man leave his father and his mother, and shall cleave unto his wife: and they shall be one."—*The Adventist Home*, p. 25, par. 3.

The Lord created every tree in Eden pleasant to the eyes and good for food, and He bade Adam and Eve freely enjoy His bounties. But He made one exception. Of the tree of knowledge of good and evil they were not to eat. This tree God reserved as a constant reminder of His ownership of all. Thus He gave them opportunity to demonstrate their faith and trust in Him by their perfect obedience to His requirements.—*Testimonies for the Church*, Vol. 6, p. 386, par. 1.

Chapter 2

MARRIAGE

God Himself gave Adam a companion. He provided "an help meet for him"—a helper corresponding to him—one who was fitted to be his companion, and who could be one with him in love and sympathy. Eve was created from a rib taken from the side of Adam, signifying that she was not to control him as the head, nor to be trampled under his feet as an inferior, but to stand by his side as an equal, to be loved and protected by him. A part of man, bone of his bone, and flesh of his flesh, she was his second self, showing the close union and the affectionate attachment that should exist in this relation. "For no man ever yet hated his own flesh; but nourisheth and cherisheth it." Ephesians 5:29. "Therefore shall a man leave his father and his mother, and shall cleave unto his wife; and they shall be one."—*Letters to Young Lovers*, p. 11, par. 2.

I have often read these words: "Marriage is a lottery." Some act as if they believed the statement, and their married life testifies that it is such to them. But true marriage is not a lottery. Marriage was instituted in Eden. After the creation of Adam, the Lord said, "It is not good that the man should be alone; I will make him an help meet"— suitable—"for him." When the Lord presented Eve to Adam, angels of God were witnesses to the ceremony. But there are few couples who are completely united when the marriage ceremony is performed. The form of words spoken over the two who take the marriage vow does not make them a unit. In their future life is to be the blending of the two in wedlock. It may be made a really happy union, if each will give to the other true heart affection.—*In Heavenly Places*, p. 203, par. 2.

"The law of the Lord is perfect, converting the soul; the testimony of the Lord is sure, making wise the simple." Before man was created, the heavenly intelligences were governed by the principles of the law of God. When man was created, God gave to Adam and Eve a knowledge of his ten precepts. When the morning stars sang together, and all the sons of God shouted for joy, God laid the foundation for marriage and for the Sabbath institution. In their happy innocency, the Lord placed Adam and Eve in the Garden of Eden, and gave them employment in dressing and keeping the garden which he had made for them. In activity of body and mind they had the means of obtaining good, and of glorifying their Heavenly Father. Like the angels of God, who are ever engaged in doing good, in carrying out God's commands, man was ever to engage in earnest work.—"Man's Relation to the Law," *The Signs of the Times*, 10-8-94, par. 1.

He who gave Eve to Adam as a helpmeet performed His first miracle at a marriage festival. In the festal hall where friends and kindred rejoiced together, Christ began His public ministry. Thus He sanctioned marriage, recognizing it as an institution that He Himself had established. He ordained that men and women should be united in holy wedlock, to rear families whose members, crowned with honor, should be recognized as members of the family above.—*The Adventist Home*, p. 99, par. 3.

A neglect on the part of woman to follow God's plan in her creation, an effort to reach for important positions which He has not qualified her to fill, leaves vacant the position that she could fill to acceptance. In getting out of her sphere, she loses true womanly dignity and nobility. When God created Eve, He designed that she should possess neither inferiority nor superiority to the man, but that in all things she should be his equal. The holy pair were to have no interest independent of each other; and yet each had an individuality in thinking and acting. But after Eve's sin, as she was first in the transgression, the Lord told her that Adam should rule over her. She was to be in subjection to her husband, and this was a part of the curse. In many cases the curse has made the lot of woman very grievous and her life a burden. The superiority which God has given man he has abused in many respects by exercising arbitrary power. Infinite wisdom devised the plan of redemption, which places the race on a second probation by giving them another trial.—*Testimonies for the Church*, vol. 3, p. 484, par. 1.

As it was in the days of Noah, so shall it be also in the days when the Son of man shall be revealed [see Luke 17:26, 20]. One of the most marked features of the earth's inhabitants in the days of Noah was their intense worldliness. They made eating and drinking, buying and selling, marrying and giving in marriage, the supreme objects of life. It is not sinful, but the fulfillment of a duty, to eat and drink, if that which is lawful is not carried to excess. And in the days of Noah it was lawful to marry. God Himself instituted marriage when He gave Eve to Adam.—*Manuscript Releases*, vol. 19, p.246, par. 4.

God made from man a woman, to be a companion and helpmeet for him, to be one with him, to cheer, encourage, and bless him. And he in his turn is to be her strong helper. All who enter the matrimonial life with a holy purpose, the husband to obtain the pure affection of a woman's heart, the wife to soften and improve her husband's character, and give it completeness, fulfil God's purpose for them. Christ came not to destroy the law, but to fulfil its every specification. He came to pull down and destroy the works of oppression that the enemy had raised up everywhere. It was in perfect harmony with His character and work to make known the fact that marriage is a holy institution. He came not to destroy this institution, but to restore it to its original sanctity. He came to restore the moral image of God in man, and He began His work by sanctioning the marriage relation. Thus He who made the first holy pair, and who created for them a paradise, put His seal upon the institution first celebrated in Eden, when the morning stars sang together, and all the sons of God shouted for joy.—"The Marriage in Cana of Galilee," *The Signs of the Times*, 9-6-99, par. 12.

When the Pharisees afterward questioned Him concerning the lawfulness of divorce, Jesus pointed His hearers back to the marriage institution as ordained at creation. "Because of the hardness of your hearts," He said, Moses "suffered you to put away your wives: but from the beginning it was not so." He referred them to the blessed days of Eden when God pronounced all things "very good." Then marriage and the Sabbath had their origin, twin institutions for the glory of God in the benefit of humanity. Then, as the Creator joined the hands of the holy pair in wedlock, saying, A man shall "leave his father and his mother, and shall cleave unto his wife: and they shall be one," He enunciated the law of marriage for all the children of Adam to the close of time. That which the eternal Father Himself had pronounced good was the law of highest blessing and development for man.—*The Adventist Home*, p. 340, par. 4.

Thus marriage was instituted. God himself united the holy pair; and this first marriage is an example of what all marriages should be. God gave the man one wife. Had he deemed it best for man to have more than one wife, he could as easily have given him two; but he sanctioned no such thing. Wherever polygamy is practised, it is against our Heavenly Father's wise arrangement. Under this practise the race degenerates, and all that makes married life elevated and ennobling is blasted.—"Marriages, Wise and Unwise," *The Youth's Instructor*, 8-10-99, art: , par. 5.

Chapter 3

THE SABBATH

The Gospel, first given to Adam in Eden, has lost none of its high claims since that time. We are required to obey all the commandments of God. The Sabbath commandment is placed in the midst of the Decalogue, and it was instituted in Eden at the same time that God instituted the marriage relation. God gave the Sabbath as a memorial of his creative power and works, "for in six days the Lord made heaven and earth, the sea, and all that in them is, and rested the seventh day; wherefore the Lord blessed the Sabbath day, and hallowed it." He made its observance obligatory upon man, in order that he might contemplate the works of God, dwell upon his goodness, his mercy, and love, and through nature look up to nature's God. If man had always observed the Sabbath, there would never have been an unbeliever, and infidel, or an atheist in the world. If Adam and Eve had contemplated the works of God in creating the world, if they had considered the reason that God had in giving them the Sabbath, if they had looked upon the beautiful tokens he had given them in withholding nothing that would add to their happiness, they would have been safe, they would have adored him for his goodness and love toward them, and in place of listening to the sophistries of Satan in casting blame upon God, in ascribing to him motives of selfishness, they would have considered the works of his hands, and songs of melody and thanksgiving and praise would have burst forth from their lips in adoration of him who had bountifully supplied them with every good thing. If they had considered how he had made them the object of his overflowing love, they would not have fallen; but they forgot the presence of God. They forgot that angels surrounded them to guard them from every danger, and they looked away from their great

Benefactor.—"The Test of Loyalty," *The Signs of the Times,* 2-13-96, par. 7.

Every one is tested and tried in probationary time in regard to his obedience to the word of God. But what is the matter with the professed Christian world?—That which was the matter with Adam and Eve in Eden,—they are listening to another voice than that of God. God's voice, which is speaking plainly and distinctly to them through the fourth commandment, is disregarded; and a false voice, which advocates a false Sabbath, is listened to. They turn from a plain, "Thus saith the Lord," to a Sabbath based upon inference and supposition, without a particle of Scriptural evidence to support it. Satan has succeeded in throwing the Christian world off the track, as he threw Adam and Eve off. People are walking in by and forbidden paths. O, why are men, when tempted, so easily overcome? Why are they so deceived in regard to the Sabbath? Why, without any foundation for their faith, do they accept and exalt a spurious Sabbath?—"God's Holy Sabbath," *Advent Review and Sabbath Herald,* 7-6-97, par. 8.

Adam was commanded to teach his descendants the fear of the Lord, and, by his example and humble obedience, teach them to highly regard the offerings which typified a Saviour to come. Adam carefully treasured what God had revealed to him, and handed it down by word of mouth to his children and children's children. By this means the knowledge of God was preserved. There were some righteous upon the earth who knew and feared God even in Adam's day. The Sabbath was observed before the fall. Because Adam and Eve disobeyed God's command, and ate of the forbidden fruit, they were expelled from Eden; but they observed the Sabbath after their fall. They had experienced the bitter fruits of disobedience, and learned that every transgressor of God's commands will sooner or later learn that God means just what he says, and that he will surely punish the transgressor.—*The Spirit of Prophecy,* Vol. 1, p. 59, par. 1.

I was shown that the law of God would stand fast forever, and exist in the new earth to all eternity. At the creation, when the foundations of the earth were laid, the sons of God looked with admiration upon the work of the Creator, and all the heavenly host shouted for joy. It was then that the foundation of the Sabbath was laid. At the close of the six days of creation, God rested on the seventh day from all His work which He had made; and He blessed the seventh day and sanctified it, because that in it He had rested from all His work. The Sabbath was instituted in Eden before the fall, and was observed by Adam and Eve, and all the heavenly host. God rested on the seventh day, and blessed and hallowed it. I saw that the Sabbath never will be done away; but that the redeemed saints, and all the angelic host, will observe it in honor of the great Creator to all eternity.—*Early Writings*, p. 217, par. 2.

In all this, Satan is the master spirit. He has no particular regard for Sunday, but he desires that his will shall be obeyed, rather than the will of God. It was Satan that incited Adam and Eve to transgress the command of their Maker, and he has continued this work even to our own day. We see the success of his attacks upon the law of God, in the wide-spread disregard for the ancient Sabbath of Jehovah, and the well-nigh universal veneration for the institution of heathenism and papacy. And we see the terrible results, in the skepticism which everywhere prevails. The Sabbath was instituted in Eden, as a memorial of creation. It points men directly to the true God as the Maker of the heavens and the earth. Thus it stands as a mighty barrier against idolatry, atheism, and infidelity. Had the Sabbath been universally kept, not one of these evils could have gained a foot-hold in our world. There could not have been an infidel nor an idolater.—"Obedience Better Than Sacrifice," *The Signs of the Times*, 9-14-82, par 4.

All who advocate truth in distinction to error have a special work to do in vindicating the law of God. Men inspired by a power from beneath have considered it their duty to uphold as the Sabbath of the Lord the first day of the week. By thus disregarding the claim of God, ministers who claim to preach the gospel are echoing the words told to Adam and

Eve in Eden, that if they transgressed the law they would not die, but would be as gods, knowing good and evil. By their influence and example, these false shepherds have caused a lie to be received as a truth. With persevering energy they have laboured to establish a spurious sabbath, and this man-made institution has received the homage of the greater part of the world. But this does not make a day holy which God has given us as a common working day. Though this error be hoary with age, though the world bow in reverence to it, it still remains an error and a delusion; for God says, "To the law and to the testimony; if they speak not according to this word, it is because there is no light in them." Isa. 8:20.—"Upholding God's Law," *Bible Echo*, 7-27-96, par. 1.

The Sabbath was instituted in Eden and observed by our first parents before the fall. Because Adam and Eve disobeyed God's command, and ate of the forbidden fruit, they were expelled from Eden; but they observed the Sabbath after their fall. They had experienced the bitter fruits of disobedience, and learned what every one who tramples upon God's commands will sooner or later learn, that God means just what he says, and that he will surely punish the transgressor. Those who venture to lightly esteem the day upon which Jehovah rested, the day which he sanctified and blessed, the day which he has commanded to be kept holy, will yet know that all the precepts of his law are alike sacred, and that death is the penalty of the transgression.—"The Great Controversy," *The Signs of the Times*, 2-6-79, par. 15.

At the very beginning of the fourth precept God said, "Remember," knowing that man, in the multitude of his cares and perplexities, would be tempted to excuse himself from meeting the full requirements of the law, or in the press of worldly business would forget its sacred importance. It is not the first day, or any common day, but the seventh that God has blessed and set apart for a sacred use. As he surveyed his work of creation, he saw that it was very good, and he rested on that day. And he designed that man should keep it holy because he himself on that day had rested. The teachers of our day, however high their claims to sanctity, who would pronounce the law of God Jewish, are wresting the Scriptures, misleading the people, and making God's law of none effect. The Sabbath was given to Adam and Eve in Eden for all their posterity. The Jews were not more closely related to Adam than were any of the other nations on the earth. Instead of losing its force now, the law is to be more fully understood. When the typical sacrifices ceased at the death of Christ, the original, as engraved on the tables of stone, stood immutable, holding its claims upon men in all ages. And in the Christian age the duty of man is not limited, but more especially defined and simply expressed.—"The Sabbath of the Fourth Commandment," *The Signs of the Times*, 7-29-97.

This worship of a false sabbath is a wedge that split the Protestant churches from God, and left them naked. They had not a text of Scripture to sustain their false god, but yet a deception, hoary with age but still a deception, was commended to reverence, and exalted, while the Sabbath of the fourth commandment was trampled upon and God dishonored. The Bible was before them with a plain "Thus saith the Lord" and the penalty that is the part of the transgressor; but as Adam and Eve in Eden listened to the falsehoods of Satan, so the righteous world are following their example.—*Manuscript Releases*, Vol. 14, p. 92, par.1.

How strange it is that the church and the world are joined together in a confederacy to do a work that God has especially prohibited! They disobey the commandments of God with impunity. The prohibition of God in the Garden of Eden was disregarded by Adam and Eve, and the most terrible consequences resulted. The Lord is placing the same test upon the human family to-day, and proving them by bringing to their attention the Sabbath, which is a memorial of God's creative power. In this memorial God testifies to the world and to heavenly intelligences that he made the world in six days, and rested—on the first day?—No, but on the seventh day. The same instruction comes to us to-day as when the Lord spoke to the children of Israel, saying, "Verily my Sabbaths ye shall keep; for it is a sign between me and you throughout your generations."—"Harmony With Apostate Powers," *The Signs of the Times*, 6-18-94, par. 7.

To Adam and Eve in Eden the Lord gave the use of every tree in the garden save one. So the Lord has given to men six days in which they are to engage in common labor; but He has put His sanctity upon the seventh day, declaring it to be holy. That day is to be sacredly observed as a memorial of creation. "God blessed the seventh day, and sanctified it; because that in it He had rested from all His work."—"The Sabbath of the Lord," *The Signs of the Times*, 3-31-98, par. 3.

Those who reverence the commandments of Jehovah, after light has been given them in reference to the fourth precept of the decalogue, will obey it without questioning the feasibility or convenience of such obedience. God made man in his own image, and then gave him an example of observing the seventh day, which he sanctified and made holy. He designed that upon that day man should worship him, and engage in no secular pursuits. No one who disregards the fourth commandment, after becoming enlightened concerning the claims of the Sabbath, can be held guiltless in the sight of God. The example of Adam and Eve in the garden should sufficiently warn us against any disobedience of the divine law.—"Cheerful Obedience Required," *Second Advent Review and Sabbath Herald*, 6-9-85, par. 15.

Hallowed by the Creator's rest and blessing, the Sabbath was kept by Adam in his innocence in holy Eden; by Adam, fallen yet repentant, when he was driven from his happy estate. It was kept by all the patriarchs, from Abel to righteous Noah, to Abraham, to Jacob. When the chosen people were in bondage in Egypt, many, in the midst of prevailing idolatry, lost their knowledge of God's law; but when the Lord delivered Israel, He proclaimed His law in awful grandeur to the assembled multitude, that they might know His will and fear and obey Him forever.—*The Great Controversy*, p.453, par. 1.

Chapter 4

THE GARDEN OF EDEN

Adam was surrounded with everything his heart could wish. Every want was supplied. There were no sin and no signs of decay in glorious Eden. Angels of God conversed freely and lovingly with the holy pair. The happy songsters caroled forth their free, joyous songs of praise to their Creator. The peaceful beasts in happy innocence played about Adam and Eve, obedient to their word. Adam was in the perfection of manhood, the noblest of the Creator's work.

Not a shadow interposed between them and their Creator. They knew God as their beneficent Father, and in all things their will was conformed to the will of God. And God's character was reflected in the character of Adam. His glory was revealed in every object of nature.—*The Adventist Home*, p. 26, par. 3, 4.

The whole natural world is designed to be an interpreter of the things of God. To Adam and Eve in their Eden home, nature was full of the knowledge of God, teeming with divine instruction. To their attentive ears it was vocal with the voice of wisdom. Wisdom spoke to the eye and was received into the heart, for they communed with God in His created works.—*Child Guidance*, p. 45, par. 3.

The home of our first parents was to be a pattern for other homes as their children should go forth to occupy the earth. That home, beautified by the hand of God Himself, was not a gorgeous palace. Men, in their pride, delight in magnificent and costly edifices, and glory in the works of their own hands: but God placed Adam in a garden. This was his dwelling. The blue heavens were its dome; the earth, with its delicate flowers and carpet of living green, was its floor; and the leafy branches of the goodly trees were its canopy. Its walls were hung with the most magnificent adornings—the handiwork of the great Master Artist. In the surroundings of the holy pair was a lesson for all time—that true happiness is found, not in the indulgence of pride and luxury, but in communion with God through His created works. If men would give less attention to the artificial and would cultivate greater simplicity, they would come far nearer to answering the purpose of God in their creation. Pride and ambition are never satisfied, but those who are truly wise will find substantial and elevating pleasure in the sources of enjoyment that God has placed within the reach of all.—*The Adventist Home*, p.132, par. 1.

Since God is the source of all true knowledge, it is, as we have seen, the first object of education to direct our minds to His own revelation of Himself. Adam and Eve received knowledge through direct communion with God; and they learned of Him through His works. All created things, in their original perfection, were an expression of the thought of God. To Adam and Eve nature was teeming with divine wisdom. But by transgression man was cut off from learning of God through direct communion and, to a great degree, through His works. The earth, marred and defiled by sin, reflects but dimly the Creator's glory. It is true that His object lessons are not obliterated. Upon every page of the great volume of His created works may still be traced His handwriting. Nature still speaks of her Creator. Yet these revelations are partial and imperfect. And in our fallen state, with weakened powers and restricted vision, we are incapable of interpreting aright. We need the fuller revelation of Himself that God has given in His written word.—*Education*, p. 16, par. 3.

The tree of life is a representation of the preserving care of Christ for His children. As Adam and Eve ate of this tree, they acknowledged their dependence upon God. The tree of life possessed the power to perpetuate life, and as long as they ate of it, they could not die. The lives of the antediluvians were protracted because of the life-giving power of this tree, which was transmitted to them from Adam and Eve.—*S.D.A. Bible Commentary*, Vol. 7, p. 988, par. 9.

While they remained true to God, Adam and his companion were to bear rule over the earth. Unlimited control was given them over every living thing. The lion and the lamb sported peacefully around them or lay down together at their feet. The happy birds flitted about them without fear; and as their glad songs ascended to the praise of their Creator, Adam and Eve united with them in thanksgiving to the Father and the Son.

The holy pair were not only children under the fatherly care of God but students receiving instruction from the all-wise Creator. They were visited by angels, and were granted communion with their Maker, with no obscuring veil between. They were full of the vigor imparted by the tree of life, and their intellectual power was but little less than that of the angels. The mysteries of the visible universe—"the wondrous works of Him which is perfect in knowledge" (Job 37:16)—afforded them an exhaustless source of instruction and delight. The laws and operations of nature, which have engaged men's study for six thousand years, were opened to their minds by the infinite Framer and Upholder of all. They held converse with leaf and flower and tree, gathering from each the secrets of its life. With every living creature, from the mighty leviathan that playeth among the waters to the insect mote that floats in the sunbeam, Adam was familiar. He had given to each its name, and he was acquainted with the nature and habits of all. God's glory in the heavens, the innumerable worlds in their orderly revolutions, "the balancings of the clouds," the mysteries of light and sound, of day and night—all were open to the study of our first parents. On every leaf of the forest or stone of the mountains, in every shining star, in earth and air and sky, God's name was written. The order and harmony of creation spoke to them of infinite wisdom and power. They were ever discovering some attraction that filled their hearts with deeper love and called forth fresh expressions of gratitude.—*Patriarchs and Prophets*, p. 50, par. 2, 3.

The Garden of Eden, the home of our first parents, was exceedingly beautiful. Graceful shrubs and delicate flowers greeted the eye at every turn. In the garden were trees of every variety, many of them laden with fragrant and delicious fruit. On their branches the birds caroled their songs of praise. Adam and Eve, in their untainted purity, delighted in the sights and sounds of Eden. And today, although sin has cast its shadow over the earth, God desires His children to find delight in the works of His hands. To locate our sanitariums amidst the scenes of nature would be to follow God's plan, and the more closely this plan is followed, the more wonderfully will He work to restore suffering humanity. For our educational and medical institutions, places should be chosen where, away from the dark clouds of sin that hang over the great cities, the Sun of Righteousness can arise, "with healing in His wings." Malachi 4:2.—*Counsels on Health*, p.266, par. 1.

In Eden each day's labor brought to Adam and Eve health and gladness, and the happy pair greeted with joy the visits of their Creator, as in the cool of the day He walked and talked with them. Daily God taught them His lessons.—*Manuscript Releases*, Vol. 17, p. 351, par. 3.

Before sin entered our world through the transgression of God's law, it was the glory of Adam and Eve to obey God's requirements. They lived in perfect conformity to his will. Not a cloud rested upon their minds to obscure their view of God. There was no doubt or uncertainty in regard to their moral obligations, and all the strength of their affections was given to their heavenly Father. A beautiful soft light, proceeding from God, enshrouded the holy pair, and was reflected from every object upon which they looked. God was their teacher, and in the beauties of nature around them his lessons were repeated. The invisible things of God were clearly seen and understood by the things which he had made.—"The True Light," *The Signs of the Times*, 1-28-97, par. 1.

Adam and Eve were charmed with the beauties of their Eden home. They were delighted with the little songsters around them, wearing their bright yet graceful plumage, and warbling forth their happy, cheerful music. The holy pair united with them and raised their voices in harmonious songs of love, praise and adoration, to the Father and his dear Son, for the tokens of love which surrounded them. They recognized the order and harmony of creation, which spoke of wisdom and knowledge that were infinite. Some new beauty and additional glory of their Eden home they were continually discovering, which filled their hearts with deeper love, and brought from their lips expressions of gratitude and reverence to their Creator.—*The Spirit of Prophecy*, Vol. 1, p.26, par. 3.

Adam and Eve could trace the skill and glory of God in every spire of grass and in every shrub and flower. The natural loveliness which surrounded them, like a mirror reflected the wisdom, excellence, and love of their heavenly Father. And their songs of affection and praise rose sweetly and reverentially to heaven, harmonizing with the songs of the exalted angels, and with the happy birds who were caroling forth their music without a care. There was no disease, decay, nor death anywhere. Life, life was in everything the eye rested upon. The atmosphere was impregnated with life....—*That I May Know Him*, p. 13, par. 5.

Adam was crowned king in Eden. To him was given dominion over every living thing that God had created. The Lord blessed Adam and Eve with intelligence such as He had not given to any other creature. He made Adam the rightful sovereign over all the works of His hands. Man, made in the divine image, could contemplate and appreciate the glorious works of God in nature.—*S.D.A. Bible Commentary*, Vol. 1, p.1082, par. 2.

Before the Fall, not a cloud rested upon the minds of our first parents to obscure their clear perception of the character of God. They were perfectly conformed to the will of God.

For a covering, a beautiful light, the light of God, surrounded them. The Lord visited the holy pair, and instructed them through the works of His hands. Nature was their lesson book. In the Garden of Eden the existence of God was demonstrated in the objects of nature that surrounded them. Every tree of the garden spoke to them. The invisible things of God were clearly seen, being understood by the things which were made, even His eternal power and Godhead.—*Selected Messages*, Book 1, p. 290, par. 2.

The holy pair looked upon nature as a picture of unsurpassed loveliness. The brown earth was clothed with a carpet of living green, diversified with an endless variety of self-propagating, self-perpetuating flowers. Shrubs, flowers, and trailing vines, regaled the senses with their beauty and fragrance. The many varieties of lofty trees were laden with fruit of every kind, and of delicious flavor, adapted to please the taste and meet the wants of the happy Adam and Eve. This Eden home God provided for our first parents, giving them unmistakable evidences of his great love and care for them.—"Redemption No. 1," *Second Advent Review and Sabbath Herald*, 2-24-72, par. 5.

Chapter 5

STATURE AND APPEARANCE

The Lord made man upright in the beginning. He was created with a perfectly balanced mind, the size and strength of all its organs being perfectly developed. Adam was a perfect type of man. Every quality of mind was well proportioned, each having a distinctive office, and yet all dependent one upon another for the full and proper use of any one of them.—*Testimonies for the Church*, Vol. 3, p. 72, par. 1.

Created to be "the image and glory of God," Adam and Eve had received endowments not unworthy of their high destiny. Graceful and symmetrical in form, regular and beautiful in feature, their countenances glowing with the tint of health and the light of joy and hope, they bore in outward resemblance the likeness of their Maker.—*My Life Today*, p. 126, par. 7.

As Adam came forth from the hand of his Creator, he was of noble height, and of beautiful symmetry. He was more than twice as tall as men now living upon earth, and was well proportioned. His features were perfect and beautiful. His complexion was neither white, nor sallow, but ruddy, glowing with the rich tint of health. Eve was not quite as tall as Adam. Her head reached a little above his shoulders. She, too, was noble—perfect in symmetry, and very beautiful.—*Last Day Events*, p. 291, par. 4.

As man came forth from the hand of his Creator, he was of lofty stature and perfect symmetry. His countenance bore the ruddy tint of health and glowed with the light of life and joy. Adam's height was much greater than that of men who now inhabit the earth. Eve was somewhat less in stature; yet her form was noble, and full of beauty. The sinless pair wore no artificial garments; they were clothed with a covering of light and glory, such as the angels wear. So long as they lived in obedience to God, this robe of light continued to enshroud them.—*Patriarchs and Prophets*, p. 45, par. 3.

The white robe of innocence was worn by our first parents when they were placed by God in holy Eden. They lived in perfect conformity to the will of God. All the strength of their affections was given to their heavenly Father. A beautiful soft light, the light of God, enshrouded the holy pair. This robe of light was a symbol of their spiritual garments of heavenly innocence. Had they remained true to God it would ever have continued to enshroud them.—*Christ's Object Lessons*, p. 310, par. 4.

The Lord created man out of the dust of the earth. He made Adam a partaker of His life, His nature. There was breathed into him the breath of the Almighty, and he became a living soul. Adam was perfect in form—strong, comely, pure, bearing the image of his Maker. God gave him a companion, a wife, to share with him the beauties of nature.—*Manuscript Releases*, p. 326, par. 4.

Chapter 6

OCCUPATION

God gave Adam and Eve employment. Eden was the school for our first parents, and God was their instructor. They learned how to till the soil and to care for the things which the Lord had planted. They did not regard labor as degrading, but as a great blessing. Industry was a pleasure to Adam and Eve.—*Fundamentals of Christian Education*, p. 314, par. 1.

God is a lover of the beautiful. He has given us unmistakable evidence of this in the work of His hands. He planted for our first parents a beautiful garden in Eden. Stately trees were caused to grow out of the ground, of every description, for usefulness and ornament. The beautiful flowers were formed, of rare loveliness, of every tint and hue, perfuming the air... It was the design of God that man should find happiness in the employment of tending the things He had created, and that his wants should be met with the fruits of the trees of the garden.

To Adam was given the work of caring for the garden. The Creator knew that Adam could not be happy without employment. The beauty of the garden delighted him, but this was not enough. He must have labor to call into exercise the wonderful organs of the body. Had happiness consisted in doing nothing, man, in his state of holy innocence, would have been left unemployed. But He who created man knew what would be for his happiness; and no sooner had He created him than He gave him his appointed work. The promise of future glory, and the decree that man must toil for his daily bread, came from the same throne.—*The Adventist Home*, p. 27, par. 1, 2.

He who taught Adam and Eve in Eden how to tend the garden would instruct men today. There is wisdom for him who holds the plow and plants and sows the seed. The earth has its concealed treasures, and the Lord would have thousands and tens of thousands working upon the soil who are crowded into the cities to watch for a chance to earn a trifle....Those who will take their families into the country place them where they have fewer temptations. The children who are with parents that love and fear God are in every way much better situated to learn of the Great Teacher, who is the source and fountain of wisdom. They have a much more favorable opportunity to gain a fitness for the kingdom of heaven.—*The Adventist Home*, p. 143, par. 1.

The Lord made Adam and Eve and placed them in the Garden of Eden to dress the garden and keep it for the Lord. It was for their happiness to have some employment, or else the Lord would not have appointed them their work.

When in counsel with the Father before the world was, it was designed that the Lord God should plant a garden for Adam and Eve in Eden and give them the task of caring for the fruit trees and cultivating and training the vegetation. Useful labor was to be their safeguard, and it was to be perpetuated through all generations to the close of earth's history.—*Child Guidance*, p. 345, par. 1, 2.

Although everything God had made was in the perfection of beauty, and there seemed nothing wanting upon the earth which God had created to make Adam and Eve happy, yet He manifested His great love to them by planting a garden especially for them. A portion of their time was to be occupied in the happy employment of dressing the garden, and a portion in receiving the visits of angels, listening to their instruction, and in happy meditation. Their labor was not wearisome but pleasant and invigorating. This beautiful garden was to be their home.

In this garden the Lord placed trees of every variety for usefulness and beauty. There were trees laden with luxuriant fruit, of rich fragrance, beautiful to the eye, and pleasant to the taste, designed of God to be food for the holy pair. There were the lovely vines which grew upright, laden with their burden of fruit, unlike anything man has seen since the fall. The fruit was very large and of different colors; some nearly black, some purple, red, pink, and light green. This beautiful and luxuriant growth of fruit upon the branches of the vine was called grapes. They did not trail upon the ground, although not supported by trellises, but the weight of the fruit bowed them down. It was the happy labor of Adam and Eve to form beautiful bowers from the branches of the vine and train them, forming dwellings of nature's beautiful, living trees and foliage, laden with fragrant fruit.—*Conflict and Courage*, p. 12, par. 2, 3.

God prepared for Adam and Eve a beautiful garden. He provided for them everything their wants required. He planted for them trees of every variety, bearing fruit. With a liberal hand he surrounded them with his bounties—the trees, for usefulness and beauty, and the lovely flowers, which sprung up spontaneously, and flourished in rich profusion around them, were to know nothing of decay. Adam and Eve were rich indeed. They possessed beautiful Eden. Adam was monarch in this beautiful domain. None can question the fact that Adam was rich. But God knew that Adam could not be happy unless he had employment. Therefore he gave him something to do. He was to dress the garden.—"Proper Education," *The Health Reformer*, 5-1-73, par. 1.

Holy angels often visited the garden, and gave instruction to Adam and Eve concerning their employment and also taught them concerning the rebellion and fall of Satan...—*Early Writings*, p.147, par. 1.

To Adam and Eve was committed the care of the garden, "to dress it and to keep it." Genesis 2:15. Though rich in all that the Owner of the universe could supply, they were not to be idle. Useful occupation was appointed them as a blessing, to strengthen the body, to expand the mind, and to develop the character.—*Education*, p. 21, par. 2.

In Eden each day's labor brought to Adam and Eve health and gladness, and the happy pair greeted with joy the visits of their Creator, as in the cool of the day He walked and talked with them. Daily God taught them His lessons.—*Manuscript Releases*, Vol. 17, p. 351, par. 3.

We want men and women who can be energized by the Spirit of God to do a complete work under the Spirit's guidance. But these minds must be cultivated, employed to do thorough work, not lazy and dwarfed by inaction. Just so men and women and children are wanted who will work the land, and use their tact and skill, not with a feeling that they are menials, but that they are doing just such noble work as God gave to Adam and Eve in Eden, who love to see the miracles wrought by the Divine Husbandman. The human agent plants the seed the God waters it, and causes His sun to shine upon it, and up springs the tiny blade. Here is the lesson God gives to us concerning he resurrection of the body and the renewing of the heart. We are to learn of spiritual things from the development of the earthly....—*Manuscript Releases*, Vol. 11, p. 183, par. 2.

Adam and Eve were given the garden of Eden to care for. They were "to dress it and to keep it." They were happy in their work. Mind, heart, and will acted in perfect harmony. In their labor they found no weariness, no toil. Their hours were filled with useful work and communion with each other. Their occupation was pleasant. God and Christ visited them and talked with them. They were given perfect freedom. Only one restriction was placed on them. "Of every tree in the garden thou mayest freely eat," God said, "but of the tree of the knowledge of good and evil, thou shalt not eat of it; for in the day that thou eatest thereof thou shalt surely die" (Genesis 2:16–17).—*Manuscript Releases*, Vol. 10, p. 327, par. 1.

Education means more than the mere studying of books. It is necessary that both the physical and mental powers be exercised in order to have a proper education. When in counsel with the Father before the world was, it was designed that the Lord God should plant a garden for Adam and Eve in Eden, and give them the task of caring for the fruit trees, and cultivating and training the vegetation. Useful labor was to be their safeguard, and it was to be perpetuated through all generations to the close of earth's history. To have a whole-sided education, it is necessary to combine science with practical labor. From infancy children should be trained to do those things that are appropriate for their age and ability. Parents should now encourage their children to become more independent. Serious troubles are soon to be seen upon the earth, and children should be trained in such a way as to be able to meet them. Many parents give a great deal of time and attention to amusing their children, encouraging them to bring all their troubles to them; but children should be trained to amuse themselves, to exercise their minds in devising plans for their own satisfaction, doing the simple things that are natural for them to do.—"How Parents Should Discipline Their Children," *The Signs of the Times*, 8-13-96, par. 5.

If there are duties to be done in your domestic life, you do not think it possible that you could do them, but you depend upon others. Sometimes it is exceedingly inconvenient for you to obtain the help you need You frequently expend double the strength required to perform the task, in planning and searching for someone to do the work for you. If you would only bring your mind to do these little acts and family duties yourself, you would be blessed and strengthened in it, and your influence in the cause of God would be far greater. God made Adam and Eve in Paradise, and surrounded them with everything that was useful and lovely. He planted for them a beautiful garden. No herb nor flower nor tree was wanting which might be for use or ornament. The Creator of man knew that the workmanship of His hands could not be happy without employment. Paradise delighted their souls, but this was not enough; they must have labor to call into exercise the wonderful organs of the body. The Lord had made the organs for use. Had happiness consisted in doing nothing, man, in his state of holy innocence, would have been left unemployed. But He who formed man knew what would be for his best happiness, and He no sooner made him than He gave him his appointed work. In order to be happy, he must labor.—*Testimonies for the Church*, Vol. 3, p. 76, par. 3.

You and your wife might have saved yourselves many ill turns and been more cheerful and happy had you sought your ease less and combined physical labor with your study. Your muscles were made for use, not to be inactive. God gave to Adam and Eve in Eden all that their wants required; yet their heavenly Father knew that they needed employment in order to retain their happiness. If you, Brother R, would exercise your muscles in laboring with your hands some portion of each day, combining labor with study, your mind would be better balanced, your thoughts would be of a purer and more elevated character, and your sleep would be more natural and healthful. Your head would be less confused and stupid because of a congested brain. Your thoughts upon sacred truth would be clearer, and your moral powers more vigorous. You do not love labor; but it is for your good to have more physical exercise daily; for it will quicken the sluggish blood to healthful activity, and will carry you above discontent and infirmities.—*Testimonies for the Church*, Vol. 3, p. 235, par. 1.

Well, the school has made an excellent beginning. The students are learning how to plant trees, strawberries, etc.; how they must keep every sprangle and fiber of the roots uncramped in order to give them a chance to grow. Is not this a most precious lesson as to how to treat the human mind, and the body as well—not to cramp any of the organs of the body, but give them ample room to do their work? The mind must be called out, its energies taxed. We want men and women who can be energized by the Spirit of God to do a complete work under the Spirit's guidance. But these minds must be cultivated, employed, not lazy and dwarfed by inaction. Just so men and women and children are wanted who will work the land, and use their tact and skill, not with a feeling that they are menials, but that they are doing just such noble work as God gave to Adam and Eve in Eden, who loved to see the miracles wrought by the divine Husbandman. The human agent plants the seed, and God waters it and causes His sun to shine upon it, and up springs the tiny blade. Here is the lesson God gives to us concerning the resurrection of the body, and the renewing of the heart. We are to learn of spiritual things from the development of the earthly.—*Testimonies to Ministers*, p.242, par. 2.

Chapter 7

A WARNING AND A TEST

God assembled the angelic host to take measures to avert the threatened evil. It was decided in Heaven's council for angels to visit Eden and warn Adam that he was in danger from the foe. Two angels sped on their way to visit our first parents. The holy pair received them with joyful innocence, expressing their grateful thanks to their Creator for thus surrounding them with such a profusion of his bounty. Everything lovely and attractive was theirs to enjoy, and everything seemed wisely adapted to their wants; and that which they prized above all other blessings, was the society of the Son of God and the heavenly angels, for they had much to relate to them at every visit, of their new discoveries of the beauties of nature in their lovely Eden home, and they had many questions to ask relative to many things which they could but indistinctly comprehend.

The angels graciously and lovingly gave them the information they desired. They also gave them the sad history of Satan's rebellion and fall. They then distinctly informed them that the tree of knowledge was placed in the garden to be a pledge of their obedience and love to God; that the high and happy estate of the holy angels was to be retained upon condition of obedience; that they were similarly situated; that they could obey the law of God and be inexpressibly happy, or disobey, and lose their high estate, and be plunged into hopeless despair.

They told Adam and Eve that God would not compel them to obey—that he had not removed from them power to go contrary to his will; that they were moral agents, free to obey or disobey. There was but one prohibition that God had seen fit to lay upon them as yet. If they should transgress the will of God, they would surely die. They told Adam and Eve that the most exalted angel, next in order to Christ, refused obedience to the law of God which he had ordained to govern heavenly beings; that this rebellion had caused war in Heaven which resulted in the rebellious being expelled therefrom, and every angel was driven out of Heaven who united with him in questioning the authority of the great Jehovah; and that this fallen foe was now an enemy to all that concerned the interest of God and his dear Son.—*The Spirit of Prophecy*, Vol. 1, p. 32, 33.

God created Adam and Eve, and placed them in charge of the Garden of Eden, where everything was beautiful to look upon, and the fruit pleasant to the taste. He said to them, "Of every tree of the garden thou mayest freely eat; but of the tree of the knowledge of good and evil, thou shalt not eat of it; for in the day that thou eatest thereof thou shalt surely die." They were forbidden to eat the fruit of this tree. This seems a small thing, but it was a test of their obedience and of their trust and confidence in God. God told them that if they disobeyed, death would be the result. Their happiness depended on obedience.—"His Wonderful Love," *The Signs of the Times*, 10-10-00, par. 1.

The long-suffering of God had been waiting the development of Satan's revolt. The Creator would test man to see if he would accept the lie of Satan in place of the truth of God. The restriction placed upon man was one which, if respected, would not deprive him of a single blessing. All the angels of heaven were prepared to come to the aid of Adam and Eve in this contest with the enemy, if they would call upon God for help. An intense interest prevailed in the heavenly courts in this trial of man's obedience...—"The Enmity," *The Signs of the Times*, 2-17-09, par. 2.

Holy angels often visited the garden, and gave instruction to Adam and Eve concerning their employment and also taught them concerning the rebellion and fall of Satan. The angels warned them of Satan and cautioned them not to separate from each other in their employment, for they might be brought in contact with this fallen foe. The angels also enjoined upon them to follow closely the directions God had given them, for in perfect obedience only were they safe. Then this fallen foe could have no power over them.—*Early Writings*, p. 147, par. 1.

In the Garden of Eden was the "tree of knowledge of good and evil....And the Lord God commanded the man, saying, Of every tree of the garden thou mayest freely eat: but of the tree of the knowledge of good and evil, thou shalt not eat." Genesis 2:9–17. It was the will of God that Adam and Eve should not know evil. The knowledge of good had been freely given them; but the knowledge of evil,—of sin and its results, of wearing toil, of anxious care, of disappointment and grief, of pain and death,—this was in love withheld.—*Education*, p. 23, par. 2.

Adam and Eve were placed upon trial, that it might be demonstrated as to whether they would obey the word of their Creator, or disobey his requirements. The Creator of man was his Father, and had an entire right to the service he could render. Body, soul, and spirit, man was the sole property of God. God revealed himself to the innocent pair in Eden, and conversed with them freely. God was their teacher, and instructed them in regard to their work. He made it plain to them that by obedience to his holy law they would retain happiness, and finally be blessed with immortality. Eternal life should be theirs if they regulated their conduct according to the principles of the law of God. Man was not left in uncertainty to suppose as to what course he should pursue, or to take any risk by venturing on some line of conduct which he might think a safe course. As children are educated by faithful parents, so Adam and Eve were instructed as to what was required of them as intelligent creatures of God. Every provision was made whereby blessings might be secured to the human race, and but one mild restriction was placed upon the sinless pair to test their loyalty to God.—"Man's Relation to the Law," *The Signs of the Times*, 10-8-94, par. 2.

Angels of God visited Adam and Eve, and told them of the fall of Satan, and warned them to be on their guard. They cautioned them not to separate from each other in their employment, for they might be brought in contact with this fallen foe. If one of them were alone, they would be in greater danger than if both were together. The angels enjoined upon them to closely follow the instructions God had given them, for in perfect obedience they were safe, and this fallen foe could then have no power to deceive them. God would not permit Satan to follow the holy pair with continual temptations. He could have access to them only at the tree of knowledge of good and evil.—*Spiritual Gifts*, Vol. 3, p. 39, par 1.

The Lord did not prove Adam and Eve in a large matter. The test given them was the smallest that could have been devised. Had it been a large test, then men and women whose hearts incline to evil would excuse themselves by saying, "This is a trivial matter, and God is not so particular about little things," and there would be constant transgression in things looked upon as small, and which pass unrebuked among men. But the Lord has made it very evident that sin, in any degree, is offensive to him.—"The Test of Christian Living," *The Signs of the Times*, 10-29-85, par. 14.

Every man has been placed on trial, as were Adam and Eve in Eden. As the tree of knowledge was placed in the midst of the garden of Eden, so the Sabbath command is placed in the midst of the decalogue. In regard to the fruit of the tree of knowledge, the restriction was made, "Ye shall not eat of it,…lest ye die." Of the Sabbath, God said, Ye shall not defile it, but keep it holy. "Remember the Sabbath day, to keep it holy." As the tree of knowledge was the test of Adam's obedience, so the fourth command is the test that God has given to prove the loyalty of all his people. The experience of Adam is to be a warning to us so long as time shall last. It warns us not to receive any assurance from the mouth of men or of angels that will detract one jot or tittle from the sacred law of Jehovah.—"The Sabbath Test," *Advent Review and Sabbath Herald*, 8-30-98, par. 13.

Chapter 8

THE ADVERSARY

Adam and Eve assured the angels that they should never transgress the express command of God, for it was their highest pleasure to do His will. The angels united with Adam and Eve in holy strains of harmonious music, and as their songs pealed forth from blissful Eden, Satan heard the sound of their strains of joyful adoration to the Father and Son. And as Satan heard it his envy, hatred, and malignity increased, and he expressed his anxiety to his followers to incite them (Adam and Eve) to disobedience and at once bring down the wrath of God upon them and change their songs of praise to hatred and curses to their Maker.—*Lift Him Up*, p. 20, par. 8.

His followers were seeking him; and he aroused himself and, assuming a look of defiance, informed them of his plans to wrest from God the noble Adam and his companion Eve. If he could, in any way, beguile them to disobedience, God would make some provision whereby they might be pardoned, and then himself and all the fallen angels would be in a fair way to share with them of God's mercy. If this should fail, they could unite with Adam and Eve; for when once they should transgress the law of God, they would be subjects of God's wrath, like themselves. Their transgression would place them also, in a state of rebellion; and they could unite with Adam and Eve, take possession of Eden, and hold it as their home. And if they could gain access to the tree of life in the midst of the garden, their strength would, they thought, be equal to that of the holy angels, and even God himself could not expel them.—*The Spirit of Prophecy*, Vol. 1, p. 30, par. 4.

His angels were seeking him, their leader, to acquaint him with their decision. They will unite with him in his plans, and with him bear the responsibility, and share the consequences. Satan cast off his feelings of despair and weakness, and, as their leader, fortified himself to brave out the matter, and do all in his power to defy the authority of God and his Son. He acquainted them with his plans. If he should come boldly upon Adam and Eve and make complaints of God's own Son, they would not listen to him for a moment, but would be prepared for such an attack. Should he seek to intimidate them because of his power, so recently an angel in high authority, he could accomplish nothing. He decided that cunning and deceit would do what might or force could not.—"The Great Controversy," *The Signs of the Times*, 1-16-79, par. 13.

When Satan became fully conscious that there was no possibility of his being brought again into favor with God, his malice and hatred began to be manifest. He consulted with his angels, and a plan was laid to still work against God's government. When Adam and Eve were placed in the beautiful garden, Satan was laying plans to destroy them. In no way could this happy couple be deprived of their happiness if they obeyed God. Satan could not exercise his power upon them unless they should first disobey God and forfeit His favor. Some plan must therefore be devised to lead them to disobedience that they might incur God's frown and be brought under the more direct influence of Satan and his angels. It was decided that Satan should assume another form and manifest an interest for man. He must insinuate against God's truthfulness and create doubt whether God did mean just what He said; next, he must excite their curiosity, and lead them to pry into the unsearchable plans of God—the very sin of which Satan had been guilty—and reason as to the cause of His restrictions in regard to the tree of knowledge.—*Early Writings*, p. 146, par. 2.

Had Satan revealed himself in his real character, he would have been repulsed at once, for Adam and Eve had been warned against this dangerous foe; but he worked in the dark, concealing his purpose, that he might more effectually accomplish his object. Employing as his medium the serpent, then a creature of fascinating appearance, he addressed himself to Eve: "Hath God said, Ye shall not eat of every tree of the garden?" Genesis 3:1. Had Eve refrained from entering into argument with the tempter, she would have been safe; but she ventured to parley with him and fell a victim to his wiles. It is thus that many are still overcome. They doubt and argue concerning the requirements of God; and instead of obeying the divine commands, they accept human theories, which but disguise the devices of Satan.—*The Great Controversy*, p. 531, par. 2.

The only one who promised Adam life in disobedience was the great deceiver. And the declaration of the serpent to Eve in Eden—"Ye shall not surely die"—was the first sermon ever preached upon the immortality of the soul. Yet this declaration, resting solely upon the authority of Satan, is echoed from the pulpits of Christendom and is received by the majority of mankind as readily as it was received by our first parents. The divine sentence, "The soul that sinneth, it shall die" (Ezekiel 18:20), is made to mean: The soul that sinneth, it shall not die, but live eternally. We cannot but wonder at the strange infatuation which renders men so credulous concerning the words of Satan and so unbelieving in regard to the words of God.—*Ibid.*, p. 533, par. 2.

No longer free to stir up rebellion in heaven, Satan's enmity against God found a new field in plotting the ruin of the human race. In the happiness and peace of the holy pair in Eden he beheld a vision of the bliss that to him was forever lost. Moved by envy, he determined to incite them to disobedience, and bring upon them the guilt and penalty of sin. He would change their love to distrust and their songs of praise to reproaches against their Maker. Thus he would not only plunge these innocent beings into the same misery which he was himself enduring, but would cast dishonor upon God, and cause grief in heaven.—*Patriarchs and Prophets*, p. 52, par. 1.

Satan went alone to mature plans that would most sure-ly secure the fall of Adam and Eve. He had fears that his purposes might be defeated. And again, even if he should be successful in leading Adam and Eve to disobey the commandment of God, and thus become transgressors of his law, and no good come to himself, his own case would not be improved; his guilt would only be increased.—*The Spirit of Prophecy*, Vol. 1, p. 31, par. 2.

The history of the past shows an active, working devil. He can no more be idle than harmless. Satan was found in only one tree to endanger the safety of Adam and Eve. He planned to attract the holy pair to that one tree, that they might do the very thing God had said they should not do—eat of the tree of knowledge. There was no danger to them in approaching any other tree. How plausible his speech! He laid hold of the very arguments which he uses today,—flattery, envy, distrust, questioning, and unbelief. If Satan was so cunning at first, what must he be now after gaining an experience of many thousands of years? Yet God and holy angels, and all those who abide in obedience to all the Lord's expressed will, are wiser than he. The subtlety of Satan will not decrease, but the wisdom given to men through a living connection with the Source of all light and divine knowledge will be proportion-ate to his arts and wiles.—*Testimonies for the Church*, Vol. 5, p. 504, par. 1.

We must inquire what captain we are following, under whose banner we are standing. Satan was the first transgres-sor of the law of Jehovah. We read in the Bible how sin en-tered into the world. Satan was the first one who ever ques-tioned the holy will of God, and his very first work was to transgress God's law, and then he came to Adam and Eve in Eden, and through his temptations caused them to break the commandments of God. Satan thought to win the human family to his side that they might war against the family in heaven. It was Satan's plan to war against the God of heaven. God has a constitution and laws to govern those whom he has created, and it would be a terrible thing if any of us should be found on the wrong side, warring against the government of Heaven. There are many deceptions to lead us away from the truth. Many think that Adam and Eve were very foolish in listening to the voice of the tempter that caused their fall from the high and holy estate, yet those who criticise do the same thing. Why do not the children of Adam who find fault with him for his sin, cease themselves to transgress?—"Obedience to the Law Necessary," *Advent Review and Sabbath Herald*, 7-15-90, par. 3.

Men who have large opinions of themselves are often in error, but they will not confess this. Envy and jealousy are diseases which disorder all the faculties of the being. They originated with Satan in Paradise. After he had started on the track of apostasy, he could see many things that were objectionable. After he fell he envied Adam and Eve in their innocency. He tempted them to sin, and to become like himself, disloyal to God. Those who accept of his attributes will demerit others, misrepresent and falsify in order to build up themselves. These persons are generally incurable, and as nothing that defileth can enter heaven, they will not be there. They would criticise the angels. They would covet another's crown. They would not know what to do, or what subjects to converse upon unless they could be finding some errors, some imperfections, in others. O that such ones would be changed by following Christ. O that they would become meek and lowly of heart by learning in the school of Christ. Then they would go forth, not as missionaries for Satan, to cause disunion and alienation, but as missionaries for Christ, to be peacemakers to work with Christ in restoring, not to bruise and mangle character. Let the Holy Spirit of God come in and expel this unholy passion, which cannot in the slightest degree survive in Heaven. Let it die. Let it be crucified. Open the heart to the attributes of Christ, who was pure, holy, undefiled, without guilt.—*The Paulson Collection*, p. 358, par. 5.

In His life and lessons Christ has given a perfect exemplification of the unselfish ministry which has its origin in God. God does not live for Himself. By creating the world, and by upholding all things, He is constantly ministering for others. But Satan misrepresented God to the world, as he did to Adam and Eve. Selfishness has its origin in Satan, and just as far as it is indulged, so far are Satan's attributes cherished. But Satan charged God with his own attributes, and belief in his principles was becoming more and more widespread.— *Manuscript Releases*, Vol. 2, p. 59, par. 5.

Chapter 9

TEMPTATION

In his first display of disaffection Satan was very cunning. All he claimed was that he wanted to bring in a better order of things, to make great improvements. He led the holy pair away from God, away from their allegiance to His commandments, on the same point where thousands are tempted today and where thousands fall; that is, by their vain imaginings. True knowledge is divine. Satan insinuated into the minds of our first parents a desire for a speculative knowledge, whereby he declared they would greatly improve their condition; but in order to gain this, they must take a course contrary to God's holy will; for God would not lead them to the greatest heights. It was not God's purpose that they should obtain knowledge that had its foundation in disobedience. This was a broad field into which Satan was seeking to lead Adam and Eve, and it is the same field that he opens for the world today by his temptations.—*Testimonies for the Church*, Vol. 5, p. 502, par. 2.

Satan tempted the first Adam in Eden, and Adam reasoned with the enemy, thus giving him the advantage. Satan exercised his power of hypnotism over Adam and Eve, and this power he strove to exercise over Christ. But after the word of Scripture was quoted, Satan knew that he had no chance of triumphing.—*Mind, Character, and Personality*, Vol. 2, p. 713, par. 1.

Satan commenced his work with Eve, to cause her to disobey. She first erred in wandering from her husband, next in lingering around the forbidden tree, and next in listening to the voice of the tempter, and even daring to doubt what God had said, "In the day that thou eatest thereof thou shalt surely die." She thought that perhaps the Lord did not mean just what He said, and venturing, she put forth her hand, took of the fruit and ate. It was pleasing to the eye and pleasant to the taste. Then she was jealous that God had withheld from them what was really for their good, and she offered the fruit to her husband, thereby tempting him. She related to Adam all that the serpent had said and expressed her astonishment that he had the power of speech.—*Early Writings*, p. 147, par. 2.

It was as Eve was standing near the forbidden tree that Satan gave utterance to the query of her mind, and thus the controversy on earth was begun....Satan presented to man the bribe of attaining to a higher position, of gaining knowledge and wisdom beyond that with which their Creator had endowed them, through an act of disobedience to his divine will. Satan had lost his derived power and glory, had lost heaven through pride and ambition, for he thought to place his throne above the stars of God, and to be like the Most High; and now, at a favorable opportunity, he presents the temptation which had originated with himself, in order to lead the creatures of God to doubt divine wisdom, and to cast reflection upon divine providences. Satan did not scruple at deception in order to gain his purpose and bring shadow over the life and character of the holy pair, to cause sorrow and grief in heaven, and to thwart the purpose of God in the creation of man. Pretending to be the friend of man, he placed himself as the enemy of God, and used all his power to prove that Jehovah had made a mistake in instituting the law to regulate the conduct of his creatures. But in casting contempt upon the law of God he was only seeking to further his hellish design of bringing the human race under his own control.—"Man's Relation to the Law," *The Signs of the Times*, 10-8-94, par. 4.

"Your eyes," said Satan, pointing to the tree, "shall be opened, and ye shall be as gods,"—independent. This had been the aim of Satan; this was why he fell from his high and holy estate. Now he sought to instill the same principle into the mind of Eve. He told her that God had forbidden her to eat of the fruit, in order to show his arbitrary authority, and to keep the holy pair in a state of dependence and subjection. He told her that in the violation of this commandment, advanced light would be hers; that she would be independent, untrammeled by the will of a superior. But Satan knew, as Eve did not, the result of disobedience, for he had tried it. Whatever of misery there is in the world, whatever of physical suffering, of ingratitude, rebellion, robbery of God, and contempt and defiance of him, is the result of attempting to be independent, to secure that exaltation and homage which belong alone to God.—"The First Temptation," *The Youth's Instructor*, 7-1-97, par. 5.

Adam quite well understood that his companion had transgressed the only prohibition laid upon them as a test of their fidelity and love. Eve reasoned that the serpent said they should not surely die, and his words must be true, for she felt no signs of God's displeasure, but a pleasant influence, as she imagined the angels felt. Adam regretted that Eve had left his side; but now the deed was done. He must be separated from her whose society he had loved so well. How could he have it thus? His love for Eve was strong. And in utter discouragement he resolved to share her fate. He reasoned that Eve was a part of himself; and if she must die, he would die with her; for he could not bear the thought of separation from her. He lacked faith in his merciful and benevolent Creator. He did not think that God, who had formed him out of the dust of the ground into a living, beautiful form, and had created Eve to be his companion, could supply her place. After all, might not the words of this wise serpent be correct? Eve was before him, just as lovely and beautiful, and apparently as innocent, as before this act of disobedience. She expressed greater, higher love for him than before her disobedience, as the effects of the fruit she had eaten. He saw in her no signs of death. She had told him of the happy influence of the fruit, of her ardent love for him, and he decided to brave the consequences. He seized the fruit and quickly ate it, and, like Eve, felt not immediately its ill effects.—*The Spirit of Prophecy*, Vol. 1, p. 39, par.2.

Satan had told them that they were under restriction, under bondage to the law, and that they might be free and independent by disregarding the divine prohibition concerning the tree of the knowledge of good and evil. He informed them that they would be as the angels if they would but partake of its fruit, for they would then be able to discern both good and evil. But what angels would they be like?—Not holy angels, but like the angels who had left their first estate, who were reserved under everlasting chains unto the judgment of the great day. The holy pair had received the positive word of God in regard to what they should do, but they presumed on God's mercy...—"The Words and Works of Satan," *The Signs of the Times*, 4-28-90, par. 4.

Adam was not deceived by the serpent, as was Eve, and it was inexcusable in Adam to rashly transgress God's positive command. Adam was presumptuous because his wife had sinned. He could not see what would become of Eve. He was sad, troubled, and tempted. He listened to Eve's recital of the words of the serpent, and his constancy and integrity began to waver. Doubts arose in his mind in regard to whether God did mean just as he said....—"The Temptation of Christ," *Second Advent Review and Sabbath Herald*, 4-1-75, par. 5.

With what intense interest the whole universe watched the conflict that was to decide the position of Adam and Eve. How attentively the angels listened to the words of Satan, the originator of sin, as he placed his own ideas above the commands of God, and sought to make of none effect the law of God through his deceptive reasoning! How anxiously they waited to see if the holy pair would be deluded by the tempter, and yield to his arts! They asked themselves, Will the holy pair transfer their faith and love from the Father and Son to Satan? Will they accept his falsehoods as truth? They knew that they might refrain from taking the fruit, and obey the positive injunction of God, or they might violate the express command of their Creator.—*S.D.A. Bible Commentary*, Vol. 1, p. 1083, par. 3.

Through the temptation to indulge appetite, Adam and Eve first fell from their high, holy, and happy estate. And it is through the same temptation that the race have become enfeebled. They have permitted appetite and passion to take the throne, and to bring into subjection reason and intellect.—*Temperance*, p. 15, par. 3.

Eve had overstated the words of God's command. He had said to Adam and Eve, "But of the tree of the knowledge of good and evil thou shalt not eat of it; for in the day thou eatest thereof thou shalt surely die." In Eve's controversy with the serpent, she added the clause, "Neither shall ye touch it, lest ye die." Here the subtlety of the serpent was seen. This statement of Eve gave him advantage, and he plucked the fruit, and placed it in her hand, and used her own words, "He hath said, 'If ye touch it, ye shall die.' You see no harm comes to you from touching the fruit, neither will you receive any harm by eating it."...—"Redemption," *Second Advent Review and Sabbath Herald*, 2-24-74, par. 14.

Satan will use every subtle argument to deceive men and women as he did in Eden to deceive Adam and Eve. "Yea, hath God said, Ye shall not eat of every tree of the garden?" Satan said to Eve. "And the woman said unto the serpent, We may eat of the fruit of the trees of the garden: but of the fruit of the tree which is in the midst of the garden, God hath said, Ye shall not eat of it, neither shall ye touch it, lest ye die. And the serpent said unto the woman, Ye shall not surely die: for God doth know that in the day ye eat thereof, then your eyes shall be opened, and ye shall be as gods, knowing good and evil."—"Christ's Attitude Toward the Law," *Advent Review and Sabbath Herald*, 11-15-98, par. 9.

Chapter 10

THE FALL

Satan commenced his work with Eve, to cause her to disobey. She first erred in wandering from her husband, next, in lingering around the forbidden tree, and next in listening to the voice of the tempter, and even daring to doubt what God had said—In the day that thou eatest thereof thou shalt surely die. She thought, Perhaps it does not mean just as the Lord said. She ventured to disobey. She put forth her hand, took of the fruit, and ate. It was pleasing to the eye, and pleasant to the taste. She was jealous that God had withheld from them what was really for their good. She offered the fruit to her husband, thereby tempting him. She related to Adam all that the serpent had said, and expressed her astonishment that he had the power of speech.—*Spiritual Gifts*, Vol. 1, p. 20, par. 2.

I saw a sadness come over the countenance of Adam. He appeared afraid and astonished. A struggle appeared to be going on in his mind. He told Eve he was quite certain that this was the foe that they had been warned against. If so, that she must die. She assured him she felt no ill effects, but rather a very pleasant influence, and entreated him to eat. Adam regretted that Eve had left his side, but now the deed was done. He must be separated from her whose society he had loved so well. How could he have it thus. His love for Eve was strong. And in utter discouragement he resolved to share her fate. He seized the fruit and quickly ate it, and like Eve felt not immediately its ill effects. Adam disobeyed and fell.—*Spiritual Gifts*, Vol. 3, p. 42, par. 1.

Adam and Eve both ate of the fruit, and obtained a knowledge which, had they obeyed God, they would never have had, —an experience in disobedience and disloyalty to

God,—the knowledge that they were naked. The garment of innocence, a covering from God, which surrounded them, departed; and they supplied the place of this heavenly garment by sewing together fig-leaves for aprons.—*Conflict and Courage*, p. 17, par. 2.

Adam and Eve fell through intemperate appetite. Christ came and withstood the fiercest temptation of Satan, and, in behalf of the race, overcame appetite, showing that man may overcome. As Adam fell through appetite, and lost blissful Eden, the children of Adam may, through Christ, overcome appetite, and through temperance in all things regain Eden.—*Counsels on Diet and Foods*, p. 70, par. 1.

...If Adam and Eve had contemplated the works of God in creating the world, if they had considered the reason that God had in giving them the Sabbath, if they had looked upon the beautiful tokens he had given them in withholding nothing that would add to their happiness, they would have been safe, they would have adored him for his goodness and love toward them, and in place of listening to the sophistries of Satan in casting blame upon God, in ascribing to him motives of selfishness, they would have considered the works of his hands, and songs of melody and thanksgiving and praise would have burst forth from their lips in adoration of him who had bountifully supplied them with every good thing. If they had considered how he had made them the object of his overflowing love, they would not have fallen; but they forgot the presence of God. They forgot that angels surrounded them to guard them from every danger, and they looked away from their great Benefactor.—"The Test of Loyalty," *The Signs of the Times*, 2-13-96, par. 7.

Adam listened to the specious sophistry of Satan, and received it as truth. He had originally the wonderful gift of a sinless nature. But he listened to the falsehoods of the one who fell from his first estate. Satan exercised his hypnotism upon him, and Adam, listening to him, sinned, and thus opened the door through which the enemy could ever gain access to human beings. Adam and Eve lost the spiritual life that would have been theirs by continual endowment.—*Manuscript Releases*, Vol. 3, p. 330, par. 3.

It was by the display of supernatural power, in making the serpent his medium, that Satan caused the fall of Adam and Eve in Eden. Before the close of time he will work still greater wonders. So far as his power extends, he will perform actual miracles. Says the Scripture: "He...deceiveth them that dwell on the earth by the means of those miracles which he had power to do," not merely those which he pretends to do. Something more than mere impostures is brought to view in this scripture. But there is a limit beyond which Satan cannot go, and here he calls deception to his aid and counterfeits the work which he has not power actually to perform. In the last days he will appear in such a manner as to make men believe him to be Christ come the second time into the world. He will indeed transform himself into an angel of light. But while he will bear the appearance of Christ in every particular, so far as mere appearance goes, it will deceive none but those who, like Pharaoh, are seeking to resist the truth.—*Testimonies for the Church*, Vol. 5, p. 698, par. 1.

After Adam and Eve had yielded to the tempter, the covering of light, their garment of innocence, was taken from them. "The eyes of them both were opened, and they knew that they were naked; and they sewed fig leaves together, and made themselves aprons." In the past they had been glad to see their Creator when He came to walk and talk with them. Now in their sinfulness they were afraid to meet Him. Hearing the voice of God in the garden, they "hid themselves from the presence of the Lord God amongst the trees of the garden. And the Lord God called unto Adam, and said unto him, Where art thou; and he said, I heard thy voice in the garden, and I was afraid, because I was naked and hid myself." "Who told thee that thou wast naked?" God asked. "Hast thou eaten of the tree, whereof I commanded thee that thou shouldest not eat?"...—*Sermons and Talks*, Vol. 1, p. 319, par. 2.

Adam and Eve listened to the voice of the tempter, and sinned against God. The light, the garments of heavenly innocence, departed from these tried, deceived souls, and in parting with the garments of innocence, they drew about them the dark robes of ignorance of God. The clear and perfect light of innocence, which had hitherto surrounded them, had lightened everything which they approached; but deprived of that heavenly light, the posterity of Adam could no longer trace the character of God in His created works.—*The Upward Look*, p. 198, par. 5.

Satan made his exulting boasts to Christ and to loyal angels that he had succeeded in gaining a portion of the angels in Heaven to unite with him in his daring rebellion. And now that he had succeeded in overcoming Adam and Eve, he claimed that their Eden home was his. He proudly boasted that the world which God had made was his dominion. Having conquered Adam, the monarch of the world, he had gained the race as his subjects, and he should now possess Eden, and make that his head-quarters. And he would there establish his throne, and be monarch of the world.—"Redemption," *Second Advent Review and Sabbath Herald*, 2-24-74, par. 19.

Adam and Eve transgressed the law of God. They ate of the forbidden fruit, and were driven from Eden. We might well rejoice if this had been the only fall. But since the fall of Adam, the history of the human race has been a succession of falls.—"Overcoming as Christ Overcame," *Advent Review and Sabbath Herald*, 7-9-01, par. 4.

After Adam's transgression he at first imagined himself rising to a new and higher existence. But soon the thought of his transgression terrified him. The air, that had been of a mild and even temperature, seemed to chill the guilty pair. They had a sense of sin, and felt a dread of the future, a sense of want, a nakedness of soul. The sweet love and peace seemed removed from them, and in their place a want of something came over them that they had never experienced before. They then for the first turned their attention to the external. They had not been clothed, but were draped in light as were the heavenly angels. This light which had enshrouded them departed. To relieve the sense of nakedness which they realized, their attention was directed to seek a covering for their forms; for how could they meet the eye of God and angels unclothed.

Their crime is now before them in its true light. Their transgression of God's express command assumes a clearer character. Adam censured Eve's folly in leaving his side, and being deceived by the serpent; but they both flattered themselves that God, who had given them everything to make them happy, might yet excuse their disobedience, because of his great love to them, and that their punishment would not be so dreadful after all.—"The Great Controversy," *The Signs of the Times*, 1-23-79, par. 5, 6.

The news of man's fall spread through heaven. Every harp was hushed. The angels cast their crowns from their heads in sorrow. All heaven was in agitation. A council was held to decide what must be done with the guilty pair. The angels feared that they would put forth the hand, and eat of the tree of life, and become immortal sinners...—*Early Writings*, p.148, par. 2.

Chapter 11

TAKING RESPONSIBILITY

When God came to inquire of Adam, He laid all the blame upon Eve.—*Temperance*, p. 284, par. 1.

Adam could neither deny nor excuse his sin; but instead of manifesting penitence, he endeavored to cast the blame upon his wife, and thus upon God Himself: "The woman whom Thou gavest to be with me, she gave me of the tree, and I did eat." He who, from love to Eve, had deliberately chosen to forfeit the approval of God, his home in Paradise, and an eternal life of joy, could now, after his fall, endeavor to make his companion, and even the Creator Himself, responsible for the transgression. So terrible is the power of sin.

When the woman was asked, "What is this that thou hast done?" she answered, "The serpent beguiled me, and I did eat." "Why didst Thou create the serpent? Why didst Thou suffer him to enter Eden?"—these were the questions implied in her excuse for her sin. Thus, like Adam, she charged God with the responsibility of their fall. The spirit of self-justification originated in the father of lies; it was indulged by our first parents as soon as they yielded to the influence of Satan, and has been exhibited by all the sons and daughters of Adam. Instead of humbly confessing their sins, they try to shield themselves by casting the blame upon others, upon circumstances, or upon God—making even His blessings an occasion of murmuring against Him.—*Patriarchs and Prophets*, p. 57, par. 5, 6.

The accusation which Adam brought against Eve, "The woman whom thou gavest to be with me, she gave me of the tree, and I did eat," had no influence to save him from the result of disobedience. God said, "Because thou hast hearkened unto the voice of thy wife, and hast eaten of the tree, of which I commanded thee, saying, Thou shalt not eat of it; cursed is the ground for thy sake; in sorrow shalt thou eat of it all the days of thy life; thorns also and thistles shall it bring forth to thee."—"God's Purpose for Us," *The Signs of the Times*, 5-29-01, par. 7.

...Hearing the voice of God in the garden, they "hid themselves from the presence of the Lord God amongst the trees of the garden. And the Lord God called unto Adam, and said unto him, Where art thou; and he said, I heard thy voice in the garden, and I was afraid, because I was naked and hid myself." "Who told thee that thou wast naked?" God asked. "Hast thou eaten of the tree, whereof I commanded thee that thou shouldest not eat?" Then Adam did that which it is natural for all human beings to do. He threw the blame on someone else. "The woman whom thou gavest to be with me," he said, "she gave me of the tree, and I did eat." (See Gen. 3:7–12).—*Sermons and Talks*, p. 319, par. 2.

After Adam and Eve had partaken of the forbidden fruit, they were filled with a sense of shame and terror. At first their only thought was, how to excuse their sin before God, and escape the dreaded sentence of death. When the Lord inquired concerning their sin, Adam replied, laying the guilt partly upon God, and partly upon his companion: "The woman whom thou gavest to be with me, she gave me of the tree, and I did eat." The woman put the blame upon the serpent, saying, "The serpent beguiled me, and I did eat." Why did you make the serpent? Why did you suffer him to come into Eden? These were the questions implied in her excuse for her sin, thus charging God with the responsibility of their fall. The spirit of self-justification originated in the father of lies, and has been exhibited by all the sons and daughters of Adam. Confessions of this order are not inspired by the divine Spirit, and will not be acceptable before Heaven. True repentance will lead men to bear their guilt themselves, and acknowledge it without deception or hypocrisy. Like the poor publican, not lifting up so much as their eyes unto heaven, they will smite upon their breast and cry, "God be merciful to me a sinner," and those who do not acknowledge their guilt, will be justified; for Jesus will plead his blood in behalf of the repentant soul.—"Acceptable Confession," *The Signs of the Times*, 3-16-88, par. 7.

Chapter 12

THE PENALTY

I have been shown the great love and condescension of God in giving His Son to die that man might find pardon and live. I was shown Adam and Eve, who were privileged to behold the beauty and loveliness of the Garden of Eden and were permitted to eat of all the trees in the garden except one. But the serpent tempted Eve, and she tempted her husband, and they both ate of the forbidden tree. They broke God's command, and became sinners. The news spread through heaven, and every harp was hushed. The angels sorrowed, and feared lest Adam and Eve would again put forth the hand and eat of the tree of life and be immortal sinners. But God said that He would drive the transgressors from the garden, and by cherubim and a flaming sword would guard the way of the tree of life, so that man could not approach unto it and eat of its fruit, which perpetuates immortality.—*Early Writings*, p. 125, par. 2.

It had been Satan's plan to lead Adam and Eve to disobey God, receive his frown, hoping that they then would eat of the tree of life, and live in sin. But God said he would drive the transgressors from the garden. Angels were immediately commissioned to guard the way of the tree of life, that they might gain no access to it. As Adam and Eve hear the sound of God's majestic approach, they seek to hide themselves from his inspection, whom they delighted while in their innocence and holiness, to meet.—*Spiritual Gifts*, Vol. 3, p. 44, par. 3.

Adam and Eve and their posterity lost their right to the tree of life because of their disobedience. "And the Lord God said, Behold, the man is become as one of Us, to know good and evil: and now, lest he put forth his hand, and take also of the tree of life, and eat, and live forever: therefore the Lord God sent him forth from the Garden of Eden, to till the ground from whence he was taken." Adam and Eve transgressed the law of God. This made it necessary for them to be driven from Eden and be separated from the tree of life, to eat of which after their transgression would perpetuate sin. "So He drove out the man; and He placed at the east of the Garden of Eden cherubims, and a flaming sword which turned every way, to keep the way of the tree of life." Man was dependent upon the tree of life for immortality, and the Lord took these precautions lest men should eat of that tree "and live forever"—become immortal sinners.—*Testimonies to Ministers*, p. 133, par. 3.

But what did Adam, after his sin, find to be the meaning of the words, "In the day that thou eatest thereof thou shalt surely die"? Did he find them to mean, as Satan had led him to believe, that he was to be ushered into a more exalted state of existence? Then indeed there was great good to be gained by transgression, and Satan was proved to be a benefactor of the race. But Adam did not find this to be the meaning of the divine sentence. God declared that as a penalty for his sin, man should return to the ground whence he was taken: "Dust thou art, and unto dust shalt thou return." Verse 19. The words of Satan, "Your eyes shall be opened," proved to be true in this sense only: After Adam and Eve had disobeyed God, their eyes were opened to discern their folly; they did know evil, and they tasted the bitter fruit of transgression.—*The Great Controversy*, p. 532, par. 2.

But measures were immediately taken in Heaven to defeat Satan in his plans. Strong angels, with beams of light representing flaming swords turning in every direction, were placed as sentinels to guard the way of the tree of life from the approach of Satan and the guilty pair. Adam and Eve had forfeited all right to their beautiful Eden home, and were now expelled from it. The earth was cursed because of Adam's sin, and was ever after to bring forth briers and thorns. Adam was to be exposed to the temptations of Satan while he lived, and was to finally pass through death to dust again.—"Redemption," *Second Advent Review and Sabbath Herald*, 2-24-74, par. 20.

Adam and Eve were informed that they must lose their Eden home. They had yielded to Satan's deception, and believed that God would lie. By their transgression they had opened a way for Satan to gain access to them more readily, and it was not safe for them to remain in the garden of Eden, lest in their state of sin they gain access to the tree of life, and perpetuate a life of sin. They entreated to be permitted to remain, although they acknowledged that they had forfeited all right to blissful Eden. They promised that they would in the future yield implicit obedience to God. They were informed that in their fall from innocence to guilt, they had gained no strength, but great weakness. They had not preserved their integrity while they were in a state of holy, happy innocence, and they would have far less strength to remain true and loyal in a state of conscious guilt. At these words the unhappy pair were filled with keenest anguish and remorse. They now realized that the penalty of sin was death.—"The Great Controversy, The Temptation and Fall," *The Signs of the Times*, 1-30-79, par. 12.

Many regard the punishment of Adam's transgression as too severe a penalty for so small a sin. The enemy of all righteousness has blinded the eyes of sinners, so that sin does not appear sinful. Their standard of what constitutes sin is vastly different from God's standard. Should those who regard Adam's sin as a matter of very small consequence look a little deeper, they would see the great mercy of God in giving Adam the smallest possible test. It could scarcely be called a self-denial on his part to refrain from partaking of the fruit of the tree of knowledge, for he already had everything necessary to supply his wants. A compassionate God gave no severe test, no strong temptation that would tax human endurance beyond the power to resist. The fruit itself was harmless. If God had not forbidden Adam and Eve to partake of the fruit of the tree of knowledge, their action in taking it would not have been sinful. Up to the moment of God's prohibition, Adam might have eaten of the fruit of that tree without realizing any harm. But after God had said, Thou shalt not eat, the act became a crime of great magnitude. Adam had disobeyed God. In this was his sin. The very fact that Adam's trial was small, made his sin exceeding great. God tested him in that which was least, to prove him; and with the prohibition he stated that the punishment consequent upon his disobedience would be death. If Adam could not bear this smallest of tests to prove his loyalty, he surely could not have endured a stronger trial had he been taken into closer relationship with God, to bear higher responsibilities. He evidenced that God could not trust him; should he be exposed to Satan's more determined attacks, he would signally fail.—Ibid, par. 14.

Adam and Eve had chosen the knowledge of evil, and if they ever regained the position they had lost they must regain it under the unfavorable conditions they had brought upon themselves. No longer were they to dwell in Eden, for in its perfection it could not teach them the lessons which it was now essential for them to learn. In unutterable sadness they bade farewell to their beautiful surroundings and went forth to dwell upon the earth, where rested the curse of sin.—*Education*, p. 25, par. 4.

In humility and inexpressible sadness, Adam and Eve left the lovely garden wherein they had been so happy until they disobeyed the command of God. The atmosphere was changed and it was no longer unvarying as before the transgression. God clothed them with coats of skins to protect them from the sense of chilliness and then of heat to which they are exposed.—*Spiritual Gifts*, Vol. 3, p. 46, par. 1.

Satan commenced his deception in Eden. He said to Eve, "Ye shall not surely die." This was Satan's first lesson upon the immortality of the soul, and he has carried on this deception from that time to the present, and will carry it on until the captivity of God's children shall be turned. I was pointed to Adam and Eve in Eden. They partook of the forbidden tree, and then the flaming sword was placed around the tree of life, and they were driven from the garden, lest they should partake of the tree of life, and be immortal sinners. The fruit of this tree was to perpetuate immortality. I heard an angel ask, "Who of the family of Adam have passed that flaming sword, and have partaken of the tree of life?" I heard another angel answer, "Not one of the family of Adam has passed that flaming sword, and partaken of that tree; therefore there is not an immortal sinner." The soul that sinneth, it shall die an everlasting death—a death from which there will be no hope of resurrection; and then the wrath of God will be appeased.—*Early Writings*, p. 218, par. 1.

.

Chapter 13

CAUSING CONSEQUENCES

What were the words Satan spoke to Eve?—"Ye shall not surely die; for God doth know that in the day ye eat thereof, then your eyes shall be opened, and ye shall be as gods, knowing good and evil." The "evil" was disobedience to God's commands. And Adam did indeed go thru the experience of knowing evil, with all its fearful consequences.—"God's Purpose for Us," *The Signs of the Times*, 5-29-01, par. 4.

Eve was told of the sorrow and pain that must henceforth be her portion. And the Lord said, "Thy desire shall be to thy husband, and he shall rule over thee." In the creation, God had made her the equal of Adam. Had they remained obedient to God—in harmony with His great law of love—they would ever have been in harmony with each other; but sin had brought discord, and now their union could be maintained and harmony preserved only by submission on the part of the one or the other. Eve had been the first in transgression; and she had fallen into temptation by separating from her companion, contrary to the divine direction. It was by her solicitation that Adam sinned, and she was now placed in subjection to her husband. Had the principles enjoined in the law of God been cherished by the fallen race, this sentence, though growing out of the results of sin, would have proved a blessing to them; but man's abuse of the supremacy thus given him has too often rendered the lot of woman very bitter, and made her life a burden.—*The Adventist Home*, p. 115, par. 1.

The Lord visited Adam and Eve, and made known to them the consequence of their disobedience. As they hear God's majestic approach, they seek to hide themselves from his inspection, whom they delighted, while in their innocence and holiness, to meet. "And the Lord God called unto Adam, and said unto him, Where art thou? And he said, I heard thy voice in the garden, and I was afraid because I was naked, and I hid myself. And he said, Who told thee that thou wast naked? Hast thou eaten of the tree whereof I commanded thee that thou shouldest not eat?" This question was asked by the Lord, not because he needed information, but for the conviction of the guilty pair. How didst thou become ashamed and fearful?...The Lord then addressed the serpent: "Because thou has done this, thou art cursed above all cattle, and above every beast of the field: upon thy belly shalt thou go, and dust shalt thou eat all the days of thy life." As the serpent had been exalted above the beasts of the field, he should be degraded beneath them all, and be detested by man, inasmuch as he was the medium through which Satan acted. "And unto Adam he said, Because thou hast hearkened unto the voice of thy wife, and hast eaten of the tree of which I commanded thee, saying, Thou shalt not eat of it, cursed is the ground for thy sake; in sorrow shalt thou eat of it all the days of thy life; thorns also and thistles shall it bring forth to thee; and thou shalt eat the herb of the field. In the sweat of thy face shalt thou eat bread till thou return unto the ground."—*The Spirit of Prophecy*, Vol. 1, p. 42, par.3.

Since God is the source of all true knowledge, it is, as we have seen, the first object of education to direct our minds to His own revelation of Himself. Adam and Eve received knowledge through direct communion with God; and they learned of Him through His works. All created things, in their original perfection, were an expression of the thought of God. To Adam and Eve nature was teeming with divine wisdom. But by transgression man was cut off from learning of God through direct communion and, to a great degree, through His works. The earth, marred and defiled by sin, reflects but dimly the Creator's glory. It is true that His object lessons are not obliterated. Upon every page of the great volume of His created works may still be traced His handwriting. Nature still speaks of her Creator. Yet these revelations are partial and imperfect. And in our fallen state, with weakened powers and restricted vision, we are incapable of interpreting aright. We need the fuller revelation of Himself that God has given in His written word.—*Education*, p. 16, par. 3.

Adam and Eve persuaded themselves that in so small a matter as eating of the forbidden fruit there could not result such terrible consequences as God had declared. But this small matter was the transgression of God's immutable and holy law, and it separated man from God and opened the floodgates of death and untold woe upon our world. Age after age there has gone up from our earth a continual cry of mourning, and the whole creation groaneth and travaileth together in pain as a consequence of man's disobedience. Heaven itself has felt the effects of his rebellion against God. Calvary stands as a memorial of the amazing sacrifice required to atone for the transgression of the divine law. Let us not regard sin as a trivial thing.—*Steps to Christ*, p. 33, par. 1.

When Adam and Eve realized how exalted and sacred was the law of God, the transgression of which made so costly a sacrifice necessary to save them and their posterity from utter ruin, they plead to die themselves, or to let them and their posterity endure the penalty of their transgression, rather than that the beloved Son of God should make this great sacrifice. The anguish of Adam was increased. He saw that his sins were of so great magnitude as to involve fearful consequences. And must it be that Heaven's honored Commander, who had walked with him, and talked with him, while in his holy innocence, whom angels honored and worshiped, must be brought down from his exalted position to die because of his transgression. Adam was informed that an angel's life could not pay the debt. The law of Jehovah, the foundation of his government in Heaven and upon earth, was as sacred as God himself; and for this reason the life of an angel could not be accepted of God as a sacrifice for its transgression. His law was of more importance in his sight than the holy angels around his throne. The Father could not abolish nor change one precept of his law to meet man in his fallen condition. But the Son of God, who had in unison with the Father created man, could make an atonement for man acceptable to God, by giving his life a sacrifice, and bearing the wrath of his Father. Angels informed Adam that, as his transgression had brought death and wretchedness, life and immortality would be brought to light through the sacrifice of Jesus Christ.—*The Spirit of Prophecy*, Vol. 1, p. 50, par. 2.

But while it is true that God could thus be discerned in nature, this does not favor the assertion that after the Fall a perfect knowledge of God was revealed in the natural world to Adam and his posterity. Nature could convey her lessons to man in his innocence; but transgression brought a blight upon nature, and intervened between nature and nature's God. Had Adam and Eve never disobeyed their Creator, had they remained in the path of perfect rectitude, they could have known and understood God. But when they listened to the voice of the tempter, and sinned against God, the light of the garments of heavenly innocence departed from them; and in parting with the garments of innocence, they drew about them the dark robes of ignorance of God. The clear and perfect light that had hitherto surrounded them had lightened everything they approached; but deprived of that heavenly light, the posterity of Adam could no longer trace the character of God in His created works.—*Selected Messages*, Book 1, p. 290, par. 3.

The character of sin, and God's treatment of sin, are first unfolded to us in the transgression of Adam. Sin is the transgression of the law, and when Adam and Eve sinned, they opened the floodgates of woe upon our world. The promise given to Adam that the seed of the woman should bruise the serpent's head, and that it should bruise his heel, was the first proclamation of the Gospel. But while a way was provided for the forgiveness of sin, yet in no way did this provision lessen its hateful character in the sight of God, or do away with the dire consequences that would fall upon impenitent transgressors. Christ was the Lamb slain from the foundation of the world, and men could always say, "Behold the Lamb of

God, which taketh away the sin of the world."—"The Test of Loyalty," *The Signs of the Times*, 2-13-96, par. 3.

Instead of doing justice to their neighbors, they carried out their own unlawful wishes. They had a plurality of wives, which was contrary to God's wise arrangement. In the beginning God gave to Adam one wife—showing to all who should live upon the earth, his order and law in that respect. The transgression and fall of Adam and Eve brought sin and wretchedness upon the human race, and man followed his own carnal desires, and changed God's order. The more men multiplied wives to themselves, the more they increased in wickedness and unhappiness. If one chose to take the wives, or cattle, or anything belonging to his neighbor, he did not regard justice or right but if he could prevail over his neighbor by reason of strength, or by putting him to death, he did so, and exulted in his deeds of violence. They loved to destroy the lives of animals. They used them for food, and this increased their ferocity and violence, and caused them to look upon the blood of human beings with astonishing indifference.—*Conflict and Courage*, p. 36, par. 3.

Adam and Eve in Eden were noble in stature, and perfect in symmetry and beauty. They were sinless, and in perfect health. What a contrast to the human race now! Beauty is gone. Perfect health is not known. Everywhere we look we see disease, deformity, and imbecility. I inquired the cause of this wonderful degeneracy, and was pointed back to Eden. The beautiful Eve was beguiled by the serpent to eat of the fruit of the only tree of which God had forbidden them to eat, or even touch it, lest they die.—*Counsels on Diet and Foods*, p. 145, par. 1.

Satan comes to man, as he came to Christ, with his overpowering temptations to indulge appetite. He well knows his power to overcome man upon this point. He overcame Adam and Eve in Eden upon appetite, and they lost their blissful home. What accumulated misery and crime have filled our world in consequence of the fall of Adam. Entire cities have been blotted from the face of the earth because of the debasing crimes and revolting iniquity that made them a blot upon the universe. Indulgence of appetite was the foundation of all their sins.—Ibid., p. 153, par. 1.

The wretched condition of the world at the present time has been presented before me. Since Adam's fall, the race has been degenerating. Some of the reasons for the present deplorable condition of men and women, formed in the image of God, were shown me. And a sense of how much must be done to arrest, even in a degree, the physical, mental, and moral decay, caused my heart to be sick and faint. God did not create the race in its present feeble condition. This state of things is not the work of Providence, but the work of man; it has been brought about by wrong habits and abuses, by violating the laws that God has made to govern man's existence. Through the temptation to indulge appetite, Adam and Eve first fell from their high, holy, and happy estate. And it is through the same temptation that the race have become enfeebled. They have permitted appetite and passion to take the throne, and to bring into subjection reason and intellect.— *Fundamentals of Christian Education*, p. 23, par. 1.

Christ never planted the seeds of death in the system. Satan planted these seeds when he tempted Adam to eat of the tree of knowledge which meant disobedience to God. Not one noxious plant was placed in the Lord's great garden, but after Adam and Eve sinned, poisonous herbs sprang up. In the parable of the sower the question was asked the master, "Didst not thou sow good seed in thy field? from whence then hath it tares?" The master answered, "An enemy hath done this" (Matt. 13:27, 28). All tares are sown by the evil one. Every noxious herb is of his sowing, and by his ingenious methods of amalgamation he has corrupted the earth with tares.—*Selected Messages*, Book 2, p. 288, par. 2.

Through disobedience to God Adam and Eve had lost Eden, and because of sin the whole earth was cursed. But if God's people followed His instruction, their land would be restored to fertility and beauty. God Himself gave them directions in regard to the culture of the soil, and they were to co-operate with Him in its restoration. Thus the whole land, under God's control, would become an object lesson of spiritual truth. As in obedience to His natural laws the earth should produce its treasures, so in obedience to His moral law the hearts of the people were to reflect the attributes of His character.—*The Adventist Home*, p. 143, par. 2.

This is what the transgressors of God's law have done ever since the day of Adam and Eve's disobedience. They have sewed together fig leaves to cover the nakedness caused by transgression. They have worn the garments of their own devising, by works of their own they have tried to cover their sins, and make themselves acceptable with God.—*Christ's Object Lessons*, p. 311, par. 1.

These may be regarded by men as little things, but was it a little thing for Adam and Eve to eat of the fruit which God had forbidden them to eat? The smallness of the act did not avert the consequences. It was disobedience to God's commandments, and the floodgates of woe were opened upon our world. We cannot be Christians and connive at any dishonest practise or breach of trust. The Christian will not be found spending extravagantly means that he has not earned. God requires every man to be punctual, just, and without guilt in his lips or in his heart. Be righteous in all dealings with your fellow men if you would have not only the name but the character of a Christian. Those who depart from Bible principles, and vindicate their defects as righteous, have never received the true knowledge of Christ or the experience of being in truth doers of the word. There is nothing in the word of God that glosses over or excuses one phase of selfishness, one approach to overreaching or dishonesty.—*The Paulson Collection*, p. 414, par. 3.

Yielding to Satan's suggestions, our first parents opened the floodgates of evil upon the world. The questionable principles of the father and the mother of the human race influenced some of those with whom they associated. The evil that began in Paradise has extended down through the ages. Although Adam and Eve related with sorrow to their children the sad story of the Fall, their family became a divided family. Cain chose to serve Satan, Abel to serve God. Cain killed his brother Abel, because he would not follow his example.—*Manuscript Releases*, p. 237, par. 6.

Eden, the home of Adam and Eve in their purity and innocence, came from the hand of the Creator a garden of perfect beauty; but this favored pair transgressed God's command, and were driven from the lovely home that had been prepared for them. Their sin and its sad consequences were put on record for our profit, to serve as a warning to those who should live after them. In the providence of God, samples of character are given us in his word, illustrating vice and virtue, sin and righteousness. Inspired men wrote these histories, that we, viewing the characters of these good men as a whole, might copy their virtues and avoid their failures.—"A Perfect and an Imperfect Pattern," *The Youth's Instructor*, 8-6-84, par. 1.

All Heaven mourned on account of the disobedience and fall of Adam and Eve, which brought the wrath of God upon the whole human race. They were cut off from communing with God, and were plunged in hopeless misery. The law of God could not be changed to meet man's necessity, for in God's arrangement it was never to lose its force, or give up the smallest part of its claims.—*Spiritual Gifts*, Vol. 3, p. 46, par. 2.

But in the transgression of man both the Father and the Son were dishonored. Man committed sin, and sin is the transgression of the law, which is holy, just, and good. Through sin the temple of God which he had builded for his own indwelling and glory, was reduced to ruin, was fallen and in decay. Satan beguiled the holy pair to their own destruction, and introduced an element of character that was antagonistic to God and to their fellow-creatures. Before the entrance of sin, the hearts of God's children had been filled with love toward their Creator, and they were in harmony with his will; but upon yielding to the tempter a warring element began to work in the human agent. Even the earth itself shows the curse of transgression, and signs of enmity appear. Darkness covers the earth like the pall of death, and will continue to shroud the glory of God until death is swallowed up in victory.—"Character of the Law Revealed in Christ's Life," *The Signs of the Times*, 12-12-95, par. 7.

Chapter 14

LEAVING A LESSON

Satan has come down with great power to work with the children of men. Their senses are perverted by his schemes. He lends enchantment to the view which he presents to them, covering transgression with great desirableness. As he tempted Adam and Eve, saying, "Ye shall be as gods, made wise by partaking of the fruit which God has forbidden you to eat," so he tempts men and women to-day.—"The Sinner's Hope," *The Signs of the Times*, 6-27-00, par. 5.

This was the position of the human race after man divorced himself from God by transgression. Then he was no longer entitled to a breath of air, a ray of sunshine, or a particle of food. And the reason why man was not annihilated was because God so loved him that He made the gift of His dear Son that He should suffer the penalty of his transgression. Christ proposed to become man's surety and substitute, that man, through matchless grace, should have another trial—a second probation—having the experience of Adam and Eve as a warning not to transgress God's law as they did. And inasmuch as man enjoys the blessings of God in the gift of the sunshine and the gift of food, there must be on the part of man a bowing before God in thankful acknowledgment that all things come of God. Whatever is rendered back to Him is only His own who has given it.—*Faith and Works*, p. 21, par. 2.

God will test all, even as he tested Adam and Eve, to see whether they will be obedient. Our loyalty or disloyalty will decide our destiny. Since the fall of Adam, men in every age have excused themselves for sinning, charging God with their sin, saying that they could not keep his commandments. This is the insinuation Satan cast at God in heaven. But the plea, "I cannot keep the commandments," need never be present-

ed to God; for before him stands the Saviour, the marks o
the crucifixion upon his body, a living witness that the law
can be kept. It is not that men cannot keep the law, but that
they will not.—"God's Test of Obedience," *The Watchman*
2-4-08, par. 1.

Adam and Eve suffered the terrible consequences of dis
obeying the express command of God. They might have rea
soned: This is a very small sin, and will never be taken into
account. But God treated the matter as a fearful evil, and the
woe of their transgression will be felt through all time. In
the times in which we live, sins of far greater magnitude are
often committed by those who profess to be God's children
In the transaction of business, falsehoods are uttered and
acted by God's professed people that bring His frown upon
them and a reproach upon His cause. The least departure
from truthfulness and rectitude is a transgression of the law
of God. Continual indulgence in sin accustoms the person to
a habit of wrongdoing, but does not lessen the aggravated
character of the sin. God has established immutable prin
ciples, which He cannot change without a revision of His
whole nature. If the word of God were faithfully studied by
all who profess to believe the truth, they would not be dwarfs
in spiritual things. Those who disregard the requirements o
God in this life would not respect His authority were they in
heaven.—*Testimonies for the Church*, Vol. 4, p. 311, par. 4.

It is not the magnitude of the transaction that makes i
fair or unfair, honest or dishonest. It is the purpose of the
heart begotten by covetousness and selfishness, which leads
a man to overreach his neighbor in the smallest item. If temp
tation were placed in his way, and circumstances favored
he would overreach on a much larger scale. When the strict
line of duty is passed, when rectitude is sacrificed, the way is
opened to go to greater lengths. In the case of Adam it was
not the value of the fruit of which he partook which made his
sin so grievous, but it was the departure from God's require
ments, the failure to stand the test. He was found on Satan's
side when he should have been found wholly on the side o

the Lord and of Heaven. The sin of Adam and Eve consisted in their disobedience of the express command of God.—*The Judgment*, p. 16, par. 2.

There is a spurious knowledge, the knowledge of evil and sin, which has been brought into the world by the cunning of Satan. The pursuit of this knowledge is prompted by unsanctified desires, unholy aims. Its lessons are dearly bought, but many will not be convinced that they are better left unlearned. The sons and daughters of Adam are fully as inquisitive and presumptuous as was Eve. They venture, contrary to the will of God, to gain knowledge which results, as did Eve's, in the loss of Eden.—*Manuscript Releases*, Vol. 20, p. 40, par. 1.

The history of Adam and Eve's disobedience in the very beginning of this earth's history is fully given. By that one act of disobedience our first parents lost their beautiful Eden home. And it was such a little thing! We have reason to be thankful that it was not a larger matter, because if it had been, little disregards in disobedience would have been multiplied. It was the least test that God could give the holy pair in Eden.—*Child Guidance*, p. 79, par. 5.

Christ could have spread for the people a rich repast, but food prepared merely for the gratification of appetite would have conveyed no lesson for their good. Through this miracle Christ desired to teach a lesson of simplicity. If men today were simple in their habits, living in harmony with nature's laws, as did Adam and Eve in the beginning, there would be an abundant supply for the needs of the human family. But selfishness and the indulgence of appetite have brought sin and misery, from excess on the one hand, and from want on the other.—*Counsels on Diet and Foods*, p. 90, par. 4.

Moses preached a great deal on this subject, and the reason the people did not go through to the promised land was because of repeated indulgence of appetite. Nine tenths of the wickedness among the children of today is caused by intemperance in eating and drinking. Adam and Eve lost Eden through the indulgence of appetite, and we can only regain it by the denial of the same.—*Temperance*, p. 150, par. 3.

All fraud and deceit is forbidden in the word of God. Direct theft and outright falsehood are not sins into which persons of respectability are in danger of falling. It is transgression in the little things that first leads the soul away from God. By their one sin in partaking of the forbidden fruit, Adam and Eve opened the floodgates of woe upon the world. Some may regard that transgression as a very little thing; but we see that its consequences were anything but small. The angels in heaven have a wider and more elevated sphere of action than we; but right with them and right with us are one and the same thing.—*Counsels on Health*, p. 409, par. 2.

Many look on this conflict between Christ and Satan as having no special bearing on their own life; and for them it has little interest. But within the domain of every human heart this controversy is repeated. Never does one leave the ranks of evil for the service of God without encountering the assaults of Satan. The enticements which Christ resisted were those that we find it so difficult to withstand. They were urged upon Him in as much greater degree as His character is superior to ours. With the terrible weight of the sins of the world upon Him, Christ withstood the test upon appetite, upon the love of the world, and upon that love of display which leads to presumption. These were the temptations that overcame Adam and Eve, and that so readily overcome us.—*Desire of Ages*, p. 116, par. 4.

"This is my commandment, That ye love one another, as I have loved you." My dear friends, for Christ's sake take your stand on higher ground. Every feature of our faith is to be tested in the way that is the most trying. The pillars of our faith are to be tested. Sophistry will be brought in as it was to Adam and Eve. You will be strongly tempted, and unless you have firm faith in the principles of the truth for this time, you will be led astray. Look to Christ as your helper. Take him into your heart as an abiding friend. As you do this, his blessing will rest upon you in large measure. You will be kept by the power of God. The enemy will not be able to lead you to swerve from your allegiance.—*The Paulson Collection*, p. 318, par. 5.

There are dangers presented to me and serious wrongs existing in the *Review and Herald* office at Battle Creek. There are men blindfolded, as it were, handling sacred responsibilities; and if the light now being given of God is not accepted and believed and acted upon during this coming conference, men's wisdom and specious devising will be presented and accepted in your councils as the wisdom of God, when it is the counsel originated by Satan and put into the minds of men. Men will go on in their own unsanctified, unholy spirit, and, as they advance, become more self-confident, more satisfied with their unsanctified selves. They are not led by the Lord, and men's wisdom is to them like a higher form and source of good, as Satan presented to Adam and Eve. But it is the deceiving power of the enemy. The mystery of iniquity will work, clothed in angel's robes.—*The Ellen G. White 1888 Materials*, p. 1813, par. 2.

With the results of sin before them, why are not men fortified against the suggestions of the evil one? Will not our leading brethren keep God's word before them, and be diligent students of His will, that they may not fail as did Adam and Eve? Never should our God-given powers be used to hurt one of His children. Never should we become the agents of Satan to deceive others.—*Manuscript Releases*, Vol. 16, p. 9, par. 3.

If we come in contact with sinners who are hardened and bold in sin, they will seek to lead you to be as bad as themselves; but it is for you to heed the caution and the injunction of the Word of God: "If sinners entice thee, consent thou not" [Prov. 1:10]. Send up your prayers to heaven that you may be delivered from temptation. Pray, pray, and put your will on the side of God's will. Oh, be sure to pray for the Lord to give you His grace to resist the devil, who caused the fall of Adam and Eve in Eden, and [who] with all his deceptive power will try to make of none effect the restrictions and commandments of God.—*Manuscript Releases*, Vol. 14, p. 74, par. 1.

Shall Christ be compelled to bear continually the shameful infirmities of His people because they accept the false sentiments proceeding from the first traitor in the heavenly courts? If the angels were deceived by Lucifer's ingenious methods of misrepresenting God, if Adam and Eve were deceived by his declaration that God was withholding from them the higher education that would make them as gods, is there not danger that men today will be deceived? Please read the first chapter of Patriarchs and Prophets and see if the precious truths contained in this book are not given by the Lord to protect His people from deceptions that are urged upon them just now.—*Manuscript Releases*, Vol. 10, p. 162, par. 4.

Jesus says, "Him that cometh to Me I will in no wise cast out." Then, my sister, dismiss the enemy. Tell him that you will not dishonor God by doubting His mercy, His goodness, His love. Never argue with Satan; for he has wonderful powers of deception. If, when he went to Adam and Eve, they had kept repeating the words of God, saying, "He hath said, and I believe His word, I will not distrust Him," they would not have been overcome.—*Manuscript Releases*, Vol. 8, p. 441, par. 4.

How strange it is that the church and the world are joined together in a confederacy to do a work that God has especially prohibited! They disobey the commandments of God with impunity. The prohibition of God in the Garden of Eden was disregarded by Adam and Eve, and the most terrible consequences resulted. The Lord is placing the same test upon the human family to-day, and proving them by bringing to their attention the Sabbath, which is a memorial of God's creative power. In this memorial God testifies to the world and to heavenly intelligences that he made the world in six days, and rested—on the first day?—No, but on the seventh day. The same instruction comes to us to-day as when the Lord spoke to the children of Israel, saying, "Verily my Sabbaths ye shall keep; for it is a sign between me and you throughout your generations."—"Harmony With Apostate Powers," *The Signs of the Times*, 6-18-94, par. 7.

The sinner may plead he has been doing good in most things, but in order not to be out of harmony with the world, he did not obey the fourth commandment, but kept the day the world observed. He has on the whole obeyed more than he has disregarded the commandments of God. Would this reasoning stand approved before the courts of Jehovah? What would it have availed in the case of Adam and Eve? They might have pleaded that their sin was only one little departure from God. They had obeyed him fully up to that time. They could have found excuses more plausible than men can frame to-day; but the way God dealt with them should teach the sons and daughters of Adam how he will deal with them if they break one of the least of his requirements.—"The Necessity of Obedience and Faith," *The Signs of the Times*, 12-15-87, par. 7.

There is a right side and a wrong side. Let each ask himself the question, On which side am I standing? Those who do not choose the side of Christ range themselves under the banner of darkness, with the great apostate, who in heaven refused to obey God, and who in the Garden of Eden deceived the holy pair, and opened the flood-gates of woe upon our world.—"The Right Side and the Wrong Side," *The Signs of the Times*, 6-20-00, par. 1.

One step from the path in which God has ordained us to walk, places us where we are subject to the temptations of Satan. This is represented in the case of Adam and Eve. Outside of God's way, we may be led to believe a lie. But angels of God will commune with those who obey His laws. Let mind and heart be united in following in the light that God has given. Keep soul and body pure and clean and holy.

When we do those things that God has commanded in His word, angels of God will act as our teachers. Our happiness is dependent upon our living a righteous life.—"Words of Warning," *Bible Training School*, 3-1-15, par. 5.

The principles of justice required a faithful narration of facts for the benefit of all who should ever read the Sacred Record. Here we discern the evidences of divine wisdom. We are required to obey the law of God, and are not only instructed as to the penalty of disobedience, but we have narrated for our benefit and warning the history of Adam and Eve in Paradise, and the sad results of their disobedience of God's commands. The account is full and explicit. The law given to man in Eden is recorded, together with the penalty accruing in case of its disobedience. Then follows the story of the temptation and fall, and the punishment inflicted upon our erring parents. Their example is given us as a warning against disobedience, that we may be sure that the wages of sin is death, that God's retributive justice never fails, and that He exacts from His creatures a strict regard for His commandments. When the law was proclaimed at Sinai, how definite was the penalty annexed, how sure was punishment to follow the transgression of that law, and how plain are the cases recorded in evidence of that fact!—*Testimonies for the Church*, Vol. 4, p. 11, par. 3.

Satan succeeds in making many grow restless, even after they have wrestled against difficulty, and have run well for a season. He presents temptation in a new way, and under a different aspect, and places before men human honors and advantages, and they fall, as did Adam and Eve when the serpent said, "Ye shall be as gods, knowing good and evil." Stretching beyond their capacity, they seek a more exalted position; desiring the highest seat they will finally, with shame, have to take the lowest seat. They sell their souls to the enemy, that they may be lifted up, and they will find, at last, that they are slaves to the one who degrades and ruins mankind. "Let him that thinketh he standeth take heed lest he fall."—"David's Experience in Philistia," *The Signs of the Times*, 11-16-88, par. 8.

Chapter 15

RECEIVING A PROMISE

Adam and Eve, at their creation, had a knowledge of the law of God. They were acquainted with its claims upon them; its precepts were written upon their hearts. When man fell by transgression, the law was not changed, but a remedial system was established to bring him back to obedience. The promise of a Saviour was given; and sacrificial offerings pointing forward to the death of Christ as the great sin-offering, were established.—"God's Eternal Law," *The Signs of the Times*, 2-1-10, par. 1.

Adam and Eve at their creation had knowledge of the original law of God. It was imprinted upon their hearts, and they were acquainted with the claims of law upon them. When they transgressed the law of God, and fell from their state of happy innocence, and became sinners, the future of the fallen race was not relieved by a single ray of hope. God pitied them, and Christ devised the plan for their salvation by Himself bearing the guilt. When the curse was pronounced upon the earth and upon man, in connection with the curse was a promise that through Christ there was hope and pardon for the transgression of God's law. Although gloom and darkness hung, like the pall of death, over the future, yet in the promise of the Redeemer, the Star of hope lighted up the dark future. The gospel was first preached to Adam by Christ. Adam and Eve felt sincere sorrow and repentance for their guilt. They believed the precious promise of God, and were saved from utter ruin (RH April 29, 1875).—*S.D.A. Bible Commentary*, Vol. 1, p. 1084, par. 7.

Adam was commanded to teach his descendants the fear of the Lord, and, by his example and humble obedience, teach them to highly regard the offerings which typified a

Saviour to come. Adam carefully treasured what God had revealed to him, and handed it down by word of mouth to his children and children's children. By this means the knowledge of God was preserved. There were some righteous upon the earth who knew and feared God even in Adam's day. The Sabbath was observed before the fall. Because Adam and Eve disobeyed God's command, and ate of the forbidden fruit, they were expelled from Eden; but they observed the Sabbath after their fall. They had experienced the bitter fruits of disobedience, and learned that every transgressor of God's commands will sooner or later learn that God means just what he says, and that he will surely punish the transgressor.—*The Spirit of Prophecy*, Vol. 1, p. 59, par. 1.

If Adam had not transgressed the law of God, the ceremonial law would never have been instituted. The gospel of good news was first given to Adam in the declaration made to him that the seed of the woman should bruise the serpent's head; and it was handed down through successive generations to Noah, Abraham, and Moses. The knowledge of God's law, and the plan of salvation were imparted to Adam and Eve by Christ Himself. They carefully treasured the important lesson, and transmitted it by word of mouth, to their children, and children's children. Thus the knowledge of God's law was preserved.—*Selected Messages*, Book 1, p. 230, par. 3.

After Adam and Eve had sinned, they were under bondage to the law. Because of their transgression they were sentenced to suffer death, the penalty of sin. But Christ, the propitiation for our sins, declared: "I will stand in Adam's place. I will take upon myself the penalty of his sin. He shall have another trial. I will secure for him a probation. He shall have the privileges and the opportunities of a free man, and be allowed to exercise his God-given power of choice. I will postpone the day of his arraignment for trial. He shall be bound over to appear at the bar of God in the judgment."—"Christ the Propitiation for Our Sins," *Atlantic Union Gleaner*, 8-19-03, par. 1.

The Saviour's coming was foretold in Eden. When Adam and Eve first heard the promise, they looked for its speedy fulfillment. They joyfully welcomed their first-born son, hoping that he might be the Deliverer. But the fulfillment of the promise tarried. Those who first received it died without the sight. From the days of Enoch the promise was repeated through patriarchs and prophets, keeping alive the hope of His appearing, and yet He came not. The prophecy of Daniel revealed the time of His advent, but not all rightly interpreted the message. Century after century passed away; the voices of the prophets ceased. The hand of the oppressor was heavy upon Israel, and many were ready to exclaim, "The days are prolonged, and every vision faileth." Ezek. 12:22.—*The Desire of Ages*, p. 31, par. 2.

Christ's death and resurrection completed His covenant. Before this time, it was revealed through types and shadows, which pointed to the great offering to be made by the world's Redeemer, offered in promise for the sins of the world. Anciently believers were saved by the same Saviour as now, but it was a God veiled. They saw God's mercy in figures. The promise given to Adam and Eve in Eden was the gospel to a fallen race. The promise was made that the Seed of the woman should bruise the serpent's head, and it should bruise His heel. Christ's sacrifice is the glorious fulfillment of the whole Jewish economy. The Sun of Righteousness has risen. Christ our Righteousness is shining in brightness upon us.—*Manuscript Releases*, Vol. 12, p. 54, par. 2.

God had a church when Adam and Eve and Abel accepted and hailed with joy the good news that Jesus was their Redeemer. These realized as fully then as we realize now the promise of the presence of God in their midst. Whenever Enoch found one or two who were willing to hear the message he had for them, Jesus joined with them in their worship of God. In Enoch's day there were some among the wicked inhabitants of earth who believed. The Lord never yet has left His faithful few without His presence nor the world without a witness.—*Manuscript Releases*, Vol. 4, p. 293, par. 2.

To man the first intimation of redemption was communicated in the sentence pronounced upon Satan in the garden. The Lord declared, "I will put enmity between thee and the woman, and between thy seed and her seed; it shall bruise thy head, and thou shalt bruise his heel." Genesis 3:15. This sentence, uttered in the hearing of our first parents, was to them a promise. While it foretold war between man and Satan, it declared that the power of the great adversary would finally be broken. Adam and Eve stood as criminals before the righteous Judge, awaiting the sentence which transgression had incurred; but before they heard of the life of toil and sorrow which must be their portion, or of the decree that they must return to dust, they listened to words that could not fail to give them hope. Though they must suffer from the power of their mighty foe, they could look forward to final victory.—*Patriarchs and Prophets*, p. 65, par. 4.

The plan of salvation was revealed to Adam and Eve in the garden of Eden. They were made to understand how the Son of God would come and bear their sin, and redeem them from the curse of the law. But when Christ came into the world how few recognized his divinity or comprehended the nature of his work! He was not acknowledged as the Prince of life. The earth was the battle-field where the Prince of light and the prince of darkness met to contend for the fallen race. Christ had laid aside his crown and his royal robe, he had stepped down from his throne, and had clothed his divinity with humanity. For our sakes he became poor, that we through his poverty might be made rich. He came into a world all marred and scarred by the curse. He took upon him humanity that he might know the infirmities and temptations of humanity, that he might know how to help and save men. The Captain of our salvation was made perfect through suffering. Was he not perfect before?—Yes. But he was made a perfect Saviour, learning obedience by the things which he suffered, that humanity might have a perfect character and be fitted for the society of the angels of Heaven. Man was not able, in his own behalf, to meet and overcome the prince of darkness; but Christ overcame him in man's behalf and broke his power over the human race, so that through his merits they might be overcomers in their own behalf.—"It is Best to Be Christians," *The Signs of the Times*, 5-20-89, par. 8.

Man was created upright; but he fell, and was driven from the garden of Eden, with the sentence of death pronounced upon him. The sorrow and anguish that cannot be expressed took possession of his soul. But hope was held out before him through the merits of the promised Messiah. The Son of God, who had so lovingly conversed with Adam and Eve in Eden, volunteered to take upon himself the wrath of the Father, and die in the sinner's stead. He would take from his lips the bitter cup that man was to drink, and give in its place the cup of blessing.—"The Cross of Christ," *The Signs of the Times*, 11-3-87, par. 5.

Chapter 16

THE SECOND ADAM

Christ bore the sins of the whole world. He was the second Adam. Taking upon Himself human nature, He passed over the ground where Adam stumbled and fell. Having taken humanity, He has an intense interest in human beings. He felt keenly the sinfulness, the shame, of sin. He is our Elder Brother. He came to prove that human beings can, through the power of God, live sinless lives.—"Wounded for Our Transgressions" *The Signs of the Times*, 8-9-05, par. 8.

Christ is called the second Adam. In purity and holiness, connected with God, and beloved by God, He began where the first Adam began. But the first Adam was in every way more favorably situated than Christ. The wonderful provision made in Eden for the holy pair was made by a God who loved them. Everything in nature was pure and undefiled. Fruits, flowers, and beautiful, lofty trees flourished in the garden of Eden. With everything that Adam and Eve required, they were abundantly supplied. But Satan came, and insinuated doubts of God's wisdom. He accused Him, their heavenly Father and Sovereign, of selfishness, because to test their loyalty, He had prohibited them from eating the fruit of the tree of knowledge. Eve fell under the temptation, and Adam accepted the forbidden fruit from his wife's hand. He fell under the smallest test that the Lord could devise to prove his obedience; and the floodgates of woe were opened upon our world. He was furnished with a holy nature, sinless, pure, undefiled; but he fell because he listened to the suggestions of the enemy; and his posterity became depraved. By one man's disobedience many were made sinners.—*Manuscript Releases*, Vol. 8, p. 39, par. 2.

When Jesus left heaven, and there left His power and glory, Satan exulted. He thought that the Son of God was placed in his power. The temptation took so easily with the holy pair in Eden, that he hoped he could with his satanic cunning and power overthrow even the Son of God, and thereby save his life and kingdom. If he could tempt Jesus to depart from the will of His Father, as he had done in his temptation with Adam and Eve, then his object would be gained.—*Selected Messages*, Book 1, p. 287, par. 2.

Adam and Eve fell through intemperate appetite. Christ came and withstood the fiercest temptation of Satan, and, in behalf of the race, overcame appetite, showing that man may overcome. As Adam fell through appetite, and lost blissful Eden, the children of Adam may, through Christ, overcome appetite, and through temperance in all things regain Eden.—*Counsels on Diet and Foods*, p. 70, par. 1.

Jesus left his royal robe and throne, and came to the world, that he might redeemed Adam's disgraceful failure. He passed over the ground where Adam fell; he endured temptations of tenfold greater power; and yet in every particular he obeyed the will of his Father. Of the scoffing Jews he could ask, "Which of you convinceth me of sin?" Adam and Eve were convinced of sin. They yielded to temptation, and in consequence of their transgression, the world has for long ages been flooded with misery. In contrast there is presented before us the life of Jesus, who, when tempted of Satan, came from the field of conflict a conqueror, pure and sinless. This victory he gained, not for himself, but for the ruined sons and daughters of Adam.—"A Perfect and an Imperfect Pattern," *The Youth's Instructor*, 8-6-84, par.3.

I will try to answer this important question: As God He could not be tempted: but as a man He could be tempted, and that strongly, and could yield to the temptations. His human nature must pass through the same test and trial Adam and Eve passed through. His human nature was created; it did not even possess the angelic powers. It was human, identical with our own. He was passing over the ground where Adam fell. He was now where, if He endured the test and trial in behalf of the fallen race, He would redeem Adam's disgraceful failure and fall, in our own humanity.—*Selected Messages*, Book 3, p. 129, par. 3.

The divine nature, combined with the human, made Him capable of yielding to Satan's temptations. Here the test to Christ was far greater than that of Adam and Eve, for Christ took our nature, fallen but not corrupted, and would not be corrupted unless He received the words of Satan in the place of the words of God. To suppose He was not capable of yielding to temptation places Him where He cannot be perfect example for man, and the force and the power of this part of Christ's humiliation, which is the most eventful, is no instruction or help to human beings.—*Manuscript Releases*, Vol. 16, p. 182, par. 3.

Satan tempted the first Adam in Eden, and Adam reasoned with the enemy, thus giving him the advantage. Satan exercised his power of hypnotism over Adam and Eve, and this power he strove to exercise over Christ. But after the word of Scripture was quoted, Satan knew that he had no chance of triumphing (Letter 159, 1903).—*S.D.A. Bible Commentary*, Vol. 5, p. 1081, par. 4.

The Son of God, who is the express image of the Father's person, became man's Advocate and Redeemer. He humbled Himself in taking the nature of man in his fallen condition, but He did not take the taint of sin. As the second Adam He must pass over the ground where Adam fell, meet the wily foe who caused Adam and Eve's fall, and be tempted in all points as man will be tempted, and overcome every temptation in behalf of man. To Him should man look—to Him who endured the "contradiction of sinners against Himself, lest ye be wearied and faint in your minds" (Heb. 12:3). While every human being is to be loved for Christ's sake, not one is to be looked to as supreme in counsel and unerring in wisdom.—*Manuscript Releases*, Vol. 20, p. 324, par. 1.

After Satan rebelled in heaven against the law of God, he was cast out. Adam and Eve fell under his temptations, and a warfare has been going on ever since between good and evil on this earth. Christ has passed over every step of the ground where Adam failed, and he has gained the victory in behalf of humanity. We are to be partakers of the sufferings of Christ, and to share his glory. Our trials need not make us unhappy. We need not trust to feeling; for feeling has nothing to do with our religion. The promises of God are "yea and amen in Christ Jesus," and our feelings do not alter the case in heaven. We are to live by faith.—"We Should Glorify God," *Advent Review and Sabbath Herald*, 4-30-89, par. 11.

What the law demanded of Adam and Eve in Eden, and what it demanded of Christ, the second Adam, it demands of every human being. I call upon those who profess to believe the truth to reach a higher standard. I present before you Jesus, the Majesty of heaven, who left the royal courts, and for our sake became poor, that through His poverty we might be made rich. Look at the scenes in His life of suffering. Think of His agony in Gethsemane, when, oppressed by the powers of darkness, He prayed, "Father, if it be possible, let this cup pass from me." See Him betrayed by Judas, forsaken by His disciples, condemned by priests and rulers, and delivered by Pilate to a shameful death. All this He endured that man might be elevated and ennobled, and by partaking of the divine nature, be exalted to the right hand of God.—"The Influence of the Truth," *Advent Review and Sabbath Herald*, 2-26-01, par. 14.

Christ took humanity upon Himself, that as a substitute and surety, He might act in behalf of humanity. He came to earth to bear the test that Adam failed to endure. Satan thought that this was his opportunity. United with the religious nation, the apostate strove to overcome God in Jesus Christ, to banish pure and undefiled religion from the earth. From the desert to the cross, temptation came to Christ like a tempest. As the fierceness of Satan's efforts to wound the Saviour's heel with his poisonous fangs increased, the lower Christ stepped down in the path of humiliation, self-denial, and self-sacrifice. Satan approached Christ as he approached Adam and Eve in Eden, but he failed in his purpose. Said Christ, "The prince of this world cometh, and hath nothing in Me" [John 14:30].—*Manuscript Releases*, Vol. 12, p. 404, par. 3.

When Christ had fasted for forty days and forty nights, the enemy came, tempting him to make bread of the stones. Christ knew that he would be assailed upon appetite, for it was upon this point that Adam and Eve had failed. And with the terrible weight of the sins of the world upon him, he withstood the fearful test upon appetite, upon the love of the world, and upon that love of display that leads to presumption. He endured these temptations, and overcame in man's behalf, working out for him a righteous character, because he knew that man could not do this of himself.—"Temptation—What Is It?," *The Signs of the Times*, 5-27-97, par. 6.

We have reason for ceaseless gratitude to God that Christ, by His perfect obedience, has won back the heaven that Adam lost through disobedience. Adam sinned, and the children of Adam share his guilt and its consequences; but Jesus bore the guilt of Adam, and all the children of Adam that will flee to Christ, the second Adam, may escape the penalty of transgression. Jesus regained heaven for man by bearing the test that Adam failed to endure; for He obeyed the law perfectly, and all who have a right conception of the plan of redemption will see that they cannot be saved while in transgression of God's holy precepts. They must cease to transgress the law and lay hold on the promises of God that are available for us through the merits of Christ.—*Faith and Works*, p. 88, par. 3.

All that was lost by the first Adam will be restored by the second. The prophet says, "O Tower of the flock, the strong hold of the daughter of Zion, unto Thee shall it come, even the first dominion." And Paul points forward to the "redemption of the purchased possession."—*The Adventist Home*, p. 540, par. 2.

Chapter 17

REDEMPTION

The sin of Adam and Eve had divorced earth from Heaven, and finite man from the infinite God, but Christ had passed over the very ground where Adam had failed, and at every step he was a conqueror. Every victory he gained elevated humanity in the scale of moral value before Heaven. It was impossible for man to redeem himself, and this was the reason that Jesus took human nature upon himself, that through humanity his divine nature might reach and lift up humanity.—"Christ's Comforting Assurance," *The Signs of the Times*, 6-17-89, par. 8.

The scheme of redemption is not a common study. Had it been, so many souls would not have been disloyal to God. Commencing with the apostasy and the gospel presented to Adam and Eve in Eden, and tracing down prophetic history, the Word of God unfolds the plan of redemption, gathering fresh and increased evidence, until the fulness of time came, and then Christ made His advent into the world. In Christ the Deity was represented. He was the great instructor in divine philosophy. He came without display, having no outward glory to stimulate mere admiration, and possessing no earthly riches.—*Spalding and Magan Collection*, p. 58, par. 3.

After the fall Christ became Adam's instructor. He acted in God's stead toward humanity, saving the race from immediate death. He took upon him the office of mediator. Adam and Eve were given a probation in which to return to their allegiance, and in this plan all their posterity were embraced.

Without the atonement of the Son of God there could have been no communication of blessing or salvation from God to man. God was jealous for the honor of His law. The transgression of that law had caused a fearful separation between God and man. To Adam in his innocence was granted communion, direct, free, and happy, with his Maker. After his transgression, God would communicate to man only through Christ and angels.—*Conflict and Courage*, p. 20, par. 6, 7.

When man was plunged in hopeless misery, when death was his portion, Christ left the majesty, splendor, and glory, of the heavenly kingdom, and humbled himself to a life of unexampled suffering and humiliation, and an ignominious death, that he might become a stepping-stone for man, that he might climb up upon his merits, and by virtue of his blood become enabled so to serve God, that he could accept his efforts to keep his broken law, and through obedience, man could thus be brought back again and reinstated in Eden, and share again in the glory that was at first given to the holy pair as they stood in the perfection of beauty, and in their holy innocence, in the garden of Eden. This was to be given back to Adam and his faithful children, who through the merits of the blood of Christ should be washed and sanctified and made worthy to be brought back to eat of the immortal fruit of the tree of life that Adam and Eve forfeited all right to by disobedience. If we then refuse to accept of Christ as our Saviour, are we in an exalted position? No, indeed; we are just where Adam and Eve were after their transgression, degraded, fallen, and without a Saviour; just where they would have remained had they not accepted Jesus Christ as their Redeemer.—"Practical Remarks," *Second Advent Review and Sabbath Herald*, 4-19-70, par. 8.

The Lord Jesus made the world. "All things were made by him; and without him was not anything made that was made. In him was life; and the life was the light of men. And the light shineth in darkness; and the darkness comprehended it not." Yet he who made all things, he who was equal with the Father, one with God, who was in the express image of his person and character, left the glory which he had with the Father before the world was, clothed his divinity with humanity, and came into our world in order that humanity might touch divinity, and divinity sanctify humanity. He came that the fallen sons and daughters of Adam might be recovered from the effects of Adam's transgression and fall, and, through his divine, uplifting power, become sons and daughters of God. He sees that the world is largely under the control of the enemy of God and man, and cannot break the spell of infatuation that is over them. Satan, who first tempted Eve in Eden, and through her caused the fall of Adam, continues his temptations, seeking by every power to retain men in disobedience. Every lying device is put into operation to misrepresent the Father and to dispute the authority of his only-begotten Son. Satan casts a hellish shadow before the world to hide God and the world's Redeemer from sight, so that if they were viewed at all, it might be through the mists and fogs of superstition, tradition, and error, and not in truth.—"Temporal Interests to Be Subordinated," *The Signs of the Times*, 3-28-95, par. 6.

The command is not, Let him that glorieth glory in himself, but in God. For sinful men, the highest consolation, the greatest cause of rejoicing, is that Heaven has given Jesus to be the sinner's Saviour. When Adam and Eve ate of the forbidden fruit, there was no hope for the sinful race; but Christ offered to take the sin upon himself. He offered to go over the ground where Adam stumbled and fell; to meet the tempter on the field of battle, and conquer him in man's behalf. Behold him in the wilderness of temptation. Forty days and forty nights he fasted, enduring the fiercest assaults of the powers of darkness. He trod the "wine-press alone; and of the people there was none with" him. It was not for himself, but that he might break the chain that held the human race in slavery to Satan. He saw that man had become so weakened by disobedience that he had not wisdom or strength to meet the wily foe, and this is why the Son of God takes upon himself man's nature, and, gaining the victory in our behalf, brings to us divine power, that, combined with human effort, will enable us to overcome.—"In What Shall We Glory?," *Advent Review and Sabbath Herald*, 3-15-87, par. 10.

After the enemy had betrayed Adam and Eve into sin, the connection between heaven and earth was severed; and had it not been for Christ, the way to heaven would never have been known by the fallen race. But "God so loved the world, that he gave his only begotten Son, that whosoever believeth in him should not perish, but have everlasting life." Christ is the mystic ladder, the base of which rests upon the earth, and whose topmost round reaches to the throne of the Infinite. The children of Adam are not left desolate and alienated from God; for through Christ's righteousness we have access unto the Father. "By me," said Christ, "if any man enter in, he shall be saved, and shall go in and out, and find pasture." Let earth be glad, let the inhabitants of the world rejoice, that Christ has bridged the gulf which sin had made, and has bound earth and heaven together. A highway has been cast up for the ransomed of the Lord. The weary and heavy laden may come unto him, and find rest to their souls. The pilgrim may journey toward the mansions that he has gone to prepare for those who love him.—"The Mystic Ladder," *Advent Review and Sabbath Herald*, 11-11-90, par. 7.

"That He might sanctify the people with His own blood," Christ "suffered without the gate." Heb. 13:12. For transgression of the law of God, Adam and Eve were banished from Eden. Christ, our substitute, was to suffer without the boundaries of Jerusalem. He died outside the gate, where felons and murderers were executed. Full of significance are the words, "Christ hath redeemed us from the curse of the law, being made a curse for us." Gal. 3:13.—*The Desire of Ages*, p. 741, par. 2.

The sin of Adam and Eve caused a fearful separation between God and man. And Christ steps in between fallen man and God, and says to man: "You may yet come to the Father; there is a plan devised through which God can be reconciled to man, and man to God; through a mediator you can approach God." And now He stands to mediate for you. He is the great High Priest who is pleading in your behalf; and you are to come and present your case to the Father through Jesus Christ. Thus you can find access to God.—*God's Amazing Grace*, p. 154, par. 2.

When Satan was thrust out of heaven, he determined to make the earth his kingdom. When he had tempted and overcome Adam and Eve, he claimed that by virtue of this conquest, the fallen race were his rightful subjects, and the world was his. By sin the human race had been alienated from God, they were brought into sympathy with Satan, and were ready to unite with him in rebellion against God's law. Christ undertook to redeem man and rescue the world from the grasp of Satan.

The law of God could not be set aside even to save lost man. The well-being of the universe demanded that the divine government should be maintained. But in His infinite love and mercy, the Creator sacrificed Himself. In His Son, God Himself bore the penalty of transgression, "that He might be just, and the justifier of him that believeth in Jesus." Thus man, redeemed from Satan's power, and brought again into harmony with God, might be restored to "the first dominion." In this world the great controversy was to be decided. The plan of redemption was to be wrought out on the very field that Satan claimed as his.—"The Plan of Redemption," *The Signs of the Times*, 11-4-08, par. 4, 5.

If the Avondale school ever becomes what the Lord is seeking to make it, the missionary effort of teachers and students will bear fruit. Both in the school and outside, willing subjects will be brought to allegiance to God. The rebellion which took place in heaven under the power of a lie, and the deception which led Adam and Eve to disobey the law of God, opened the floodgates of woe upon our world; but all who believe in Christ may become sons and daughters of God. Through the power of the truth they may be restored, and fallen man may become loyal to his Maker. The truth, peculiar in its working power, is adapted to the minds and hearts of wandering sinners. Through its influence the lost sheep may be brought back to the fold.—*Testimonies for the Church*, Vol. 6, p. 190, par. 2.

Such was the condition that existed in heaven before the disaffection of Satan. The heavenly current flowed through the universe of God without one cloud of evil to cast a shadow upon its bright waters. Everywhere spotless purity was reflected as in a mirror. And God was over all. But Satan fell. The human race were created. Adam and Eve fell. And now the Lord Jesus has himself bridged the gulf that sin has made, and the whole scheme of redemption has been put in operation to restore the moral image of God in man.—*The Ellen G. White 1888 Materials*, p. 1428, par. 1.

We want to keep the perfect Pattern before us. God was so good as to send a representation of Himself in His Son Jesus Christ, and we want to get the mind and heart to unfold and reach upward. Just as soon as Adam and Eve fell, their countenances fell at the sight of their miserableness. We may see our wretchedness, and we should pray that God will reveal our own hearts to us; but we should pray also that He will reveal Himself to us as a sin-pardoning Redeemer. Let yours be the prayer, Reveal Thyself to me, that in Thy matchless grace I may lay hold on the golden link, Christ, which has been let down from heaven to earth, that I may grasp it and be drawn upward.—*The Ellen G. White 1888 Materials*, p. 76, par. 1.

Now, I want to say to you before closing, that we have a wonderful friend in Jesus, who came to save His people from the transgression of the law. What is sin? The only definition of sin is that it is the transgression of the law. Then here is Jesus Christ, who comes right in and imparts His righteousness to us; we cannot overcome in our own strength, but by faith in Him. If you will believe on Jesus Christ, you will have Him today. You must believe that He is your Saviour now, and that He imputes to you His righteousness because He has died, and because He has been obedient unto every requirement of that transgressed law of God. If you do this, you will have a saving knowledge of Jesus Christ. Adam and Eve lost Eden because they transgressed that law, but you will lose heaven if you transgress it.—*The Ellen G. White 1888 Materials*, p. 128, par. 3.

Chapter 18

EDEN RESTORED

By the awful event of man's fall, it was Satan's purpose to make of the beautiful world God had created, a home of sin and woe. He designed to set the human race in rebellion and hostility against their Maker. But he was not left free to drag them down without divine interposition. The holy pair had fallen, and henceforth the earth must be marred by the curse of sin; but through the gift of the only-begotten Son of God, earth was to be restored to its Edenic purity and beauty, and man renewed in the image of God.—"The Enmity," *The Signs of the Times*, 2-17-09, par. 3.

In the earth made new the redeemed will engage in the occupations and pleasures that brought happiness to Adam and Eve in the beginning. The Eden life will be lived, the life in garden and field. "They shall build houses, and inhabit them; and they shall plant vineyards, and eat the fruit of them. They shall not build, and another inhabit; they shall not plant, and another eat: for as the days of a tree are the days of My people, and Mine elect shall long enjoy the work of their hands."—*The Adventist Home*, p. 549, par. 1.

If you cultivate faithfully the vineyard of your soul, God is making you a laborer together with Himself. And you will have a work to do not only for yourself, but for others. In representing the church as the vineyard, Christ does not teach that we are to restrict our sympathies and labors to our own numbers. The Lord's vineyard is to be enlarged. In all parts of the earth He desires it to be extended. As we receive the instruction and grace of God, we should impart to others a knowledge of how to care for the precious plants. Thus we may extend the vineyard of the Lord. God is watching for evidence of our faith, love, and patience. He looks to see if we are using every spiritual advantage to become skillful workers in His vineyard on earth, that we may enter the Paradise of God, that Eden home from which Adam and Eve were excluded by transgression.—*Christ's Object Lessons*, p. 282, par. 2.

Christ drew many of his illustrations and lessons from the great treasure house of nature. He plucked a lily and pointed His hearers to its simplicity and marvelous beauty. He pointed to the grass of the field, saying, "If God so clothe the grass of the field, which today is, and tomorrow is cast into the oven, shall He not much more clothe you?" He desires us to see that the things of nature are an expression of the love of God, and that, though marred by sin, they still speak to us of the Eden home in which Adam and Eve were placed. He desires us to be reminded by them of the time when this home shall be restored, and the earth shall be filled with the praise of the Lord.—*Evangelism*, p. 148, par. 4.

If human beings for whom Christ has died would take these words to heart and live them out in their lives, we would see a different state of things in our world today. There would be less selfishness, less love of the world, and more love for God. He has entrusted man with talents that he might carry the knowledge of the truth and of Christ to all nations in our land. If Adam and Eve had lived by every word that proceeded out of the mouth of God they never would have fallen, never lost the right to the tree of life. All who will live by every word that proceedeth out of the mouth of God now will be brought back to the Eden home.—*Manuscript Releases*, Vol. 9, p. 232, par. 1.

Adam and Eve lost all access to Eden and to the tree of life because they took the word of another before the Word of God. By this act of disobedience they opened the flood-gates of woe upon our world. But those who steadfastly adhere to God's Word, will hear the benediction, "Blessed are they that do his commandments, that they may have right to the tree of life, and may enter in through the gates into the city." No flaming sword guards that tree from those who, after the light has been given them, in the face of all opposition turn from the commandments of men to obey the commandments of God.—"We Ought to Obey God Rather Than Men," *The Signs of the Times*, 5-13-97, par. 14.

It is by grace that the sinner is saved, being justified freely by the blood of Christ. But Christ did not die to save the sinner in his sins. The whole world is condemned as guilty before God, for they are transgressors of his holy law; and they will certainly perish unless they repent, turn from their disobedience, and through faith in Christ claim the merits of his precious blood. The sin of Adam and Eve lost holy Eden for themselves and their posterity, and those who continue to live in the transgression of God's law will never regain the lost paradise. But through the grace of Christ man may render acceptable obedience, and gain a home in the beautiful Eden restored.—"Christ and the Law," *The Signs of the Times*, 7-29-86, par. 3.

The Garden of Eden remained upon the earth long after man had become an outcast from its pleasant paths. The fallen race were long permitted to gaze upon the home of innocence, their entrance barred only by the watching angels. At the cherubim-guarded gate of Paradise the divine glory was revealed. Hither came Adam and his sons to worship God. Here they renewed their vows of obedience to that law the transgression of which had banished them from Eden. When the tide of iniquity overspread the world, and the wickedness of men determined their destruction by a flood of waters, the hand that had planted Eden withdrew it from the earth. But in the final restitution, when there shall be "a new heaven and a new earth," it is to be restored more gloriously adorned than at the beginning.

Then they that have kept God's commandments shall breathe in immortal vigor beneath the tree of life; and through unending ages the inhabitants of sinless worlds shall behold, in that garden of delight, a sample of the perfect work of God's creation, untouched by the curse of sin—a sample of what the whole earth would have become had man but fulfilled the Creator's glorious plan.

God's original purpose in the creation of the earth is fulfilled as it is made the eternal abode of the redeemed. "The righteous shall inherit the land, and dwell therein for ever." The time has come to which holy men have looked with longing since the flaming sword barred the first pair from Eden—the time for "the redemption of the purchased possession." The earth originally given to man as his kingdom, betrayed by him into the hands of Satan, and so long held by the mighty foe, has been brought back by the great plan of redemption. . . . God created the earth to be the abode of holy, happy beings. That purpose will be fulfilled when, renewed by the power of God and freed from sin and sorrow, it shall become the eternal home of the redeemed.

After his expulsion from Eden Adam's life on earth was filled with sorrow. Every dying leaf, every victim of sacrifice, every blight upon the fair face of nature, every stain upon man's purity, were fresh reminders of his sin. Terrible was the agony of remorse as he beheld iniquity abounding and, in answer to his warnings, met the reproaches cast upon himself as the cause of sin. With patient humility he bore for nearly a thousand years the penalty of transgression. Faithfully did he repent of his sin and trust in the merits of the promised Saviour, and he died in the hope of a resurrection. The Son of God redeemed man's failure and fall; and now, through the work of the atonement, Adam is reinstated in his first dominion.

Transported with joy, he beholds the trees that were once his delight—the very trees whose fruit he himself had gathered in the days of his innocence and joy. He sees the vines that his own hands have trained, the very flowers that he once loved to care for. His mind grasps the reality of the scene; he comprehends that this is indeed Eden restored, more lovely now than when he was banished from it. The Saviour leads him to the tree of life and plucks the glorious fruit and bids him eat. He looks about him and beholds a multitude of his family redeemed, standing in the Paradise of God. Then he casts his glittering crown at the feet of Jesus and, falling upon

His breast, embraces the Redeemer. He touches the golden harp, and the vaults of heaven echo the triumphant song, "Worthy, worthy, worthy is the Lamb that was slain, and lives again!" The family of Adam take up the strain and cast their crowns at the Saviour's feet as they bow before Him in adoration.—*The Adventist Home*, pp. 539–541.

It is impossible to describe Adam's transports of joy as he again beholds Paradise, the garden of Eden, his once happy home, from which, because of his transgression, he had been so long separated. He beholds the lovely flowers and trees, of every description for fruit and beauty, every one of which to designate them he had named while in his innocence. He sees the luxuriant vines, which had once been his delight to train upon bowers and trees. But when he again beholds the wide spread tree of life with its extended branches and glowing fruit, and to him again is granted access to its fruit and leaves, his gratitude is boundless. He first in adoration bows at the feet of the King of glory, and then with the redeemed host swells the song, Worthy, worthy is the Lamb that was slain. Adam had lost Eden by disobeying the commandments of God. He has now regained that lovely garden by repentance and faithful obedience. The curse rested upon him for disobedience, the blessing now for his obedience.—*Spiritual Gifts*, Vol. 3, p. 89, par. 1.

All come forth from their graves the same in stature as when they entered the tomb. Adam, who stands among the risen throng, is of lofty height and majestic form, in stature but little below the Son of God. He presents a marked contrast to the people of later generations; in this one respect is shown the great degeneracy of the race. But all arise with the freshness and vigor of eternal youth. In the beginning, man was created in the likeness of God, not only in character, but in form and feature. Sin defaced and almost obliterated the divine image; but Christ came to restore that which had been lost. He will change our vile bodies and fashion them like unto His glorious body. The mortal, corruptible form, devoid of comeliness, once polluted with sin, becomes perfect, beautiful, and immortal. All blemishes and deformities are left in the grave. Restored to the tree of life in the long-lost Eden, the redeemed will "grow up" (Malachi 4:2) to the full stature of the race in its primeval glory. The last lingering traces of the curse of sin will be removed, and Christ's faithful ones will appear in "the beauty of the Lord our God," in mind and soul and body reflecting the perfect image of their Lord. Oh, wonderful redemption! long talked of, long hoped for, contemplated with eager anticipation, but never fully understood.

The living righteous are changed "in a moment, in the twinkling of an eye." At the voice of God they were glorified; now they are made immortal and with the risen saints are caught up to meet their Lord in the air. Angels "gather together His elect from the four winds, from one end of heaven to the other." Little children are borne by holy angels to their mothers' arms. Friends long separated by death are united, nevermore to part, and with songs of gladness ascend together to the City of God.

On each side of the cloudy chariot are wings, and beneath it are living wheels; and as the chariot rolls upward, the wheels cry, "Holy," and the wings, as they move, cry, "Holy," and the retinue of angels cry, "Holy, holy, holy, Lord God Almighty." And the redeemed shout, "Alleluia!" as the chariot moves onward toward the New Jerusalem.

Before entering the City of God, the Saviour bestows upon His followers the emblems of victory and invests them with the insignia of their royal state. The glittering ranks are drawn up in the form of a hollow square about their King, whose form rises in majesty high above saint and angel, whose countenance beams upon them full of benignant love. Throughout the unnumbered host of the redeemed every glance is fixed upon Him, every eye beholds His glory whose "visage was so marred more than any man, and His form more than the sons of men." Upon the heads of the overcomers, Jesus with His own right hand places the crown of glory. For each there is a crown, bearing his own "new name" (Revelation 2:17), and the inscription, "Holiness to the Lord." In every hand are placed the victor's palm and the shining harp.

Then, as the commanding angels strike the note, every hand sweeps the harp strings with skillful touch, awaking sweet music in rich, melodious strains. Rapture unutterable thrills every heart, and each voice is raised in grateful praise: "Unto Him that loved us, and washed us from our sins in His own blood, and hath made us kings and priests unto God and His Father; to Him be glory and dominion for ever and ever." Revelation 1:5, 6.

Before the ransomed throng is the Holy City. Jesus opens wide the pearly gates, and the nations that have kept the truth enter in. There they behold the Paradise of God, the home of Adam in his innocency. Then that voice, richer than any music that ever fell on mortal ear, is heard, saying: "Your conflict is ended." "Come, ye blessed of My Father, inherit the kingdom prepared for you from the foundation of the world."

Now is fulfilled the Saviour's prayer for His disciples: "I will that they also, whom Thou hast given Me, be with Me where I am." "Faultless before the presence of His glory with exceeding joy" (Jude 24), Christ presents to the Father the purchase of His blood, declaring: "Here am I, and the children whom Thou hast given Me." "Those that Thou gavest Me I have kept." Oh, the wonders of redeeming love! The rapture of that hour when the infinite Father, looking upon the ransomed, shall behold His image, sin's discord banished, its blight removed, and the human once more in harmony with the divine!

With unutterable love, Jesus welcomes His faithful ones to the joy of their Lord. The Saviour's joy is in seeing, in the kingdom of glory, the souls that have been saved by His agony and humiliation. And the redeemed will be sharers in His joy, as they behold, among the blessed, those who have been won to Christ through their prayers, their labors, and their loving sacrifice. As they gather about the great white throne, gladness unspeakable will fill their hearts, when they behold those whom they have won for Christ, and see that one has gained others, and these still others, all brought into the haven of rest, there to lay their crowns at Jesus' feet and praise Him through the endless cycles of eternity.

As the ransomed ones are welcomed to the City of God, there rings out upon the air an exultant cry of adoration. The two Adams are about to meet. The Son of God is standing with outstretched arms to receive the father of our race—the being whom He created, who sinned against his Maker, and for whose sin the marks of the crucifixion are borne upon the Saviour's form. As Adam discerns the prints of the cruel nails, he does not fall upon the bosom of his Lord, but in humiliation casts himself at His feet, crying: "Worthy, worthy is the Lamb that was slain!" Tenderly the Saviour lifts him up and bids him look once more upon the Eden home from which he has so long been exiled.

After his expulsion from Eden, Adam's life on earth was filled with sorrow. Every dying leaf, every victim of sacrifice, every blight upon the fair face of nature, every stain upon man's purity, was a fresh reminder of his sin. Terrible was the agony of remorse as he beheld iniquity abounding, and, in answer to his warnings, met the reproaches cast upon himself as the cause of sin. With patient humility he bore, for nearly a thousand years, the penalty of transgression. Faithfully did he repent of his sin and trust in the merits of the promised Saviour, and he died in the hope of a resurrection. The Son of God redeemed man's failure and fall; and now, through the work of the atonement, Adam is reinstated in his first dominion...

This reunion is witnessed by the angels who wept at the fall of Adam and rejoiced when Jesus, after His resurrection, ascended to heaven, having opened the grave for all who should believe on His name. Now they behold the work of redemption accomplished, and they unite their voices in the song of praise.—*The Great Controversy*, pp. 644–648.

And now, which example will you copy,—that of our first parents in disobeying God, or that set by the precious Saviour? The result of sin is before you, and the result of obedience. Adam lost Eden, not only for himself, but for the race,—for you and for me. But through Jesus it will be restored in more than its original loveliness. The prize before you is eternal life in the kingdom of God; is it not worth striving for? "Eye hath not seen, nor ear heard, neither have entered into the heart of man, the things that God hath prepared for them that love him." Says the psalmist, "In Thy presence is fullness of joy; at Thy right hand there are pleasures forevermore."—"A Perfect and an Imperfect Pattern," *The Youth's Instructor*, 8-6-84, par. 6.

Editor's Note: The question is sometimes raised if Eve will be in the restored Eden, as the above statements only refer to Adam. While we can only speculate, there seems to be enough evidence to support Eve's restoration as well. Consider the following:

...The gospel was first preached to Adam and Eve in Eden. They sincerely repented of their guilt, believed the promise of God, and were saved from utter ruin.—"The Law in the Patriarch Age," The Signs of the Times, 4-22-86, par. 2.

...After he [Satan] fell, he envied Adam and Eve [in] their innocence. He tempted them to sin, and they yielded, and became like himself, disloyal to God. But they repented of their sin, received Christ, and returned to their loyalty...—"The Great Controversy," *Advent Review and Sabbath Herald*, 9-14-97, par. 7.

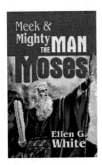

Meek and Mighty The Man Moses

A compilation of Ellen G. White's writings on the life of Moses from *The Signs of the Times* and *Patriarchs and Prophets*.

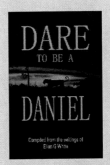

Dare to be a Daniel

A compilation of Ellen G. White's writings from *The Youth's Instructor* and other sources on the life of Daniel.

Other Titles from TEACH Services, Inc.

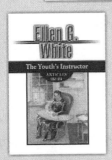

The Youth's Instructor Articles

A compilation of about 470 of Ellen G. White's articles that were originally published (1852–1914) in magazine form. Facsimile.

Christian Temperance & Bible Hygiene

This collection of writings by James and Ellen G. White will both inspire and instruct you in temperance and hygiene from a Biblical point of view.

We'd love to have you download our catalog of
titles we publish at:

www.TEACHServices.com

or write or email us your thoughts,
reactions, or criticism about this
or any other book we publish at:

TEACH Services, Inc.
254 Donovan Road
Brushton, NY 12916

info@TEACHServices.com

or you may call us at:

518/358-3494